TAME YOUR
INNER CRITIC

Challenge Your Inner Voice

Be The Person You Were

Always Meant To Be

MICHAEL GARDE

Copyright © 2020 Michael Garde All rights reserved

No part of this book may be reproduced, or stored in a retrieval system, or transmitted in any form or by any means, electronic, mechanical, photocopying, recording, or otherwise, without express written permission of the publisher.

ISBN: 9798564894746

This Book is Dedicated to:

I'm grateful to my darling wife Kerry who put up with me always being in my office, whilst writing this book, while she organised practically everything else at home. I hope someday this will all make sense to you.

To my beautiful daughters Katie, Alice and Jodie and our gorgeous grandchildren Kellum, Mason, Henry, Betsy and Florence. Proud of you all.

To my brother Ian for always believing in me from afar. I always enjoy our all too brief time together.

To my Dad, who taught me about values when growing up and led by example. You're my hero Dad.

Finally to my Mum (who sadly passed away in 2011). My Mum always believed in me and I learnt self-development from her at an early age. Love you Mum.

Thanks go to:

Michael Heppell for educating me in how to write a book and encouraging me to do so.

Fumbling Inner Critics for help and advice all along the journey.

Christine Beech for proof reading several chapters of my book. I'm afraid I'm responsible for the rest.

Steve Dobby & Fiona Setch for last minute encouragement.

Coaching Club for their support.

And special thanks go to:

You for buying this book. Thank you so much.

Table Of Contents

Introduction	6
Your Story	16
The Importance We Attach To Labels	29
Where Did My Inner Critic Come From?	42
Imposter Syndrome	57
Listening In On Your Inner Critic	68
Taming Your Inner Critic	79
Bring On Your Cheerleader	93
Your Inner Circle	105
Confidence Builder	118
Reflection	130
Quiz Question Answers	137
About The Author	141

Introduction

Remember when you were a child and the world was such an exciting place? Remember the endless possibilities, when you knew you could do and be anything you wanted?

I want you to take a moment, go back in time to when you were a child. Remember when you were young enough to dare to dream out loud? When you told the world what you wanted and who you were going to be. What did you dare to dream?

As you grew, life got a little more complex. You tried new things, and more was expected from you. Some of the things you tried worked and some did not. The ones that did not may have started sowing those first seeds of self-doubt.

I remember vividly when I was seven years old at my first school swimming lesson. Everyone was asked to jump in the pool. One by one they jumped. It came to my turn and I was excited but a little afraid too. I jumped in, and my feet slipped on the pool floor and didn't grip. I spun round underwater for what seemed like an eternity, but was in reality, about thirty seconds.

From that moment forward, I was afraid of jumping in the pool. That experience created so much self-doubt that I didn't learn to swim until I was fifteen years old. I was raised in Australia, so you can imagine what a handicap not being able to swim was.

I entered pools by the ladder from then on. My inner critic was forming and telling me for certain what would happen if I attempted to jump in the pool. As I became a father myself, I was determined that my daughters would never be fearful of the water. They had swimming lessons from a young age and I am proud to say both are brilliant swimmers. I wanted to ensure that they never had an inner critic based around the fear of water as I did.

Think about that for a moment. A mishap, lasting no more than about thirty seconds when I was seven years old, influenced my decisions as a father. What has been influencing your life from your childhood?

Another childhood memory you may relate to is learning to ride a bike. Start out on a trike, then graduate to a bike with trainer wheels. Finally, you are told it is time for the trainer wheels to come off.

One of your parents is running behind, keeping the bike steady, as you pedal away needing that initial reassurance. You keep shouting, 'Are you still holding on?' They reassure you that they are until suddenly their voice sounds a little distant. You look behind to see them in the distance and maybe you have a little wobble. Hopefully, at this stage you are confident enough to keep pedalling and - voila - you can officially ride a bike.

However, if you had a different experience and fell off, it may have knocked your confidence and started a dialogue of self-doubt. Have you ever heard the phrase 'When you fall off a horse, you have to get back in the saddle'? The meaning of the phrase is simple. Do not give your inner critic a chance to start the self-doubt dialogue. Instead, get back to what you were doing as soon as you can to rebuild your confidence before you convince yourself otherwise.

You often hear children say they can not do something. It may be because they have tried and failed, and it has knocked their confidence. Or it could be that the activity seems overwhelming. They have already started their inner dialogue, telling themselves why they can not do it. As a parent, you can guide them and help them. This way they learn that they can do many things if they persevere.

Have you ever told people you can not do something or do not like something as an adult? Is it something that is outside your comfort zone? Did you even give it a try? You may be holding yourself back from achieving great things or missing out on amazing experiences by staying within your comfort zone.

Let us revisit childhood for a moment. Social scientists seem to agree that the earliest memories you can access tend to be from the age of three to four years old. It is a real shame that you can not remember back to when you first started to walk.

Much too young to have any concept of self-doubt, you take your first tentative steps. You fall, you cry, and you get right back up again. There is an inner drive that means nothing is going to stop you from achieving this. Add to this, you usually have a parent or two as raving fans cheering you on all the way. It may take a few weeks, lots of trial and error, but eventually, you master walking, and never look back.

Imagine you had to learn to walk as an adult instead. You take the first faltering step, fall and perhaps cry. You also have a fear which babies do not. The fear of embarrassment, of failing in front of others. As an adult, there are no parents to cheer you on and your first experience of walking is a failure.

Do you give up? I think if we had to learn to walk as adults, then some of us would definitely throw in the towel. Those same people would be telling themselves they can not do it, as their inner critic goes to work, giving them all the reasons why. Fortunately, a baby has no concept of failure so just keeps going until the mission is accomplished.

As you start growing up and take on more responsibility, people's expectations of you change. Along with your own life experiences, you are also influenced by your parents, family, friends and teachers. So for example, during this time, others could start to question your career choices and bring you a little more *'down to earth'* as they see it. It is usually with the best of intentions, as they encourage you to be *'realistic'* about life and what *'they'* believe you're capable of.

Surrounded by these voices of *'reason'* it's hard not to believe these things about yourself. The same inner voice, that was so full of possibility as a child, is now starting to sound like the doubting voices from others.

Once you start to put limits on yourself, you too become part of the cycle. Unfortunately without realising it, you can start putting limits on your friends and family's dreams too.

Of course, not everyone is held back in life by their own or other's beliefs. Some with major disadvantages are now household names because they did not allow their inner critic to take over and instead they pursued their dreams.

Barack Obama, the first black president of the United States, dared to dream big.

Angela Merkel, raised in communist East Germany, went on to lead a unified Germany.

Elon Musk had an emotionally abusive childhood, but is a visionary of our time, creating both Tesla and SpaceX companies.

Oprah Winfrey, born into poverty to a single mother and molested in her childhood, is now one of the biggest media icons of our time.

Richard Branson struggled with dyslexia his whole life and created one of the world's most recognised brands.

I admire all the people above immensely for breaking through barriers and becoming icons of our time. However, to me, one man stands above them all. Nelson Mandela is my personal hero. He never let his inner critic gain control. He endured unspeakable hardships on Robben Island when he could have given up on life and society. Instead, he used every situation as a learning experience.

If you only take one thing from this book, let it be this: **Every experience in life, good or bad, is something you can learn from, to help you grow.**

Now, of course, your dreams do not have to be as grandiose as any of those above, but all these achievers were once children, and never let their dreams slip away. Isn't it time you started taking back control of your life too? I can imagine the potential in so many of you that let your dreams become distant memories. Maybe now is the time to reawaken your dreams?

As you transition into an adult, you may have new dreams and desires, but may be worried what other people will think of you if you say them out loud. Then there is always the fear of failing publicly. So your dreams are still there, but buried under the surface, as you listen to your inner critic explaining how unattainable they are.

Now you no longer control the inner dialogue, you have handed that job over to your inner critic. It can not wait to jump in and throw doubts and obstacles in your way when you want to do things outside your comfort zone. It will remind you why it is not for you and how you will feel if you fail.

I do not want this for you, I want your life to be different. I want you to be in control of attaining your dreams and destiny. One of the essential things to master is to tame your inner critic and take back control of the dialogue in your head.

To get the most out of this book, I would like you to be an active reader. By active, I mean someone who reads the information, takes part in the exercises in the book, and then digests and reflects on what they have learned. It is important to me because you have made this investment and I want you to fully invest in yourself too. I believe in you because you are reading this, and I know you would not have picked up this book if you did not want to believe in yourself too.

How should you read this book? Well ideally, from start to finish, as each chapter builds on the previous one.

Throughout this book, you will go on a journey of self-discovery. Starting from where you are now, and looking at **Your Story** in detail, possibly more than you ever have before.

You will look at **The Importance We Attach to Labels.** How if you are not careful these may define you, and how you may be defining others with labels too. Next, you will examine **Where Did My Critic Come From?** In this chapter, you will look at all the various factors that go into growing your critic, from your childhood, right through to the present day.

You may suffer from **Imposter Syndrome**? What lies behind this and how can you overcome this real fear of being found out? Fancy **Listening in on Your Inner Critic?** See what common phrases crop up for you. Once you start to notice them, you can work on them.

Taming Your Inner Critic looks at how to start taking back control by reducing the influence of your personal critic. After that, it is time to **Bring on Your Cheerleader.** You have turned down the volume of your inner critic, now drown it out by having an inner cheerleader instead.

Your Inner Circle. What influence does this have on you? How can you shape it over time, so that it reflects the person you want to be? Next up is **Confidence Builder**. How to bolster your new inner cheerleader and stack up the wins.

Reflection is the final chapter of the book. This is where you get to look back over the journey of self-discovery you have made, the exercises you have completed and reinforce your new-found purpose.

OK, now it's time for you to take some action.

Exercise 1:

I want you to imagine for a moment, that there are no doubting voices, especially in your own head.

What things would you dare to do in your life?

I want you to close your eyes and really visualise what you would love to do.

Write down all the things you would love to do.

> **Exercise 2:**
>
> I would like you to start keeping a journal of your days from this point forward, and at least until two weeks after you have finished reading this book.
>
> **I want you to write down any negative thoughts you have had throughout that day which have prevented you from doing something that you wanted or needed to do.**
>
> Capture the negative thought, along with what it has prevented you doing.
>
> Please be honest with yourself, as you will reflect on what you have written here at various stages throughout this book.

Quick Quiz:

Questions
1. If there is only one thing you take from this book, what should it be?
2. Who had an emotionally abusive childhood, but is a visionary of our time?
3. What type of reader should you be, to get the most out of this book?

Answers
1.
2.
3.

Your Story

If there is one thing that is totally unique about all of us, it is our story. No matter how similar your background is to someone else, there will always be differences. Even if it is the meaning you attach to something that someone said to you, or that happened to you.

I am not talking about the literal facts of your background - where you grew up, what schools you attended, etc. I am talking about your inner story, about all your accumulated experiences over the years and how you interpret those internally.

Let us imagine an interview situation. I am sure you will agree that most of us are nervous during these processes. Let us also call our characters Emma and Alex to make them more human. Emma and Alex are equally qualified for the role and are both accomplished professionals. They have already done well by getting to the interview stage based on their résumés. Emma is nervous but has prepared well. She overcomes her anxiety during the interview and leaves a great impression with the interviewer. Alex is nervous and has also prepared well. However during his interview, his anxiety heightens, leading him to forget things and become even more anxious as he realises that the interview is not going well. Alex appeared very anxious to the interviewer, which when combined with a less than stellar performance, does not leave the impression Alex wanted.

So how is it that some people manage to overcome their anxiety and compose themselves during an interview, yet others get overwhelmed and totally lose focus? Let's consider our two characters, and visit them the night before the interview.

Emma knows her subject well. She has rehearsed it over and over and feels confident that she is as prepared as she can be.

In the paragraphs below I will highlight our characters' inner dialogues by displaying them in this style ***"Inner dialogue style"***. These are only representative and your inner dialogue may be vastly different, since it is personal to you.

Emma's inner dialogue may go something like this:
"Have I prepared enough for this interview? I could take some pressure off myself in the morning if I get everything prepared now."
So Emma ensures that everything is laid out and ready for the next morning. She creates a checklist and goes through it, so she will not forget anything crucial, including fuel in the car. Emma asks herself:
"What else can I do to give me the best chance of success?"
Her mind searches for an answer, then she thinks:
"I can visualise the interview process, as I know top performers tend to do this."

At this point Emma visualises the interview she will be attending. She imagines going through the door, shaking the interviewer's hand and introducing herself in a confident way. She visualises the interview going well and being able to respond to all the questions in a calm, clear and professional way. Emma knows she can only do her best and that the decision of who ultimately gets the job is out of her hands. She does not focus on who else may be attending and if they may be better qualified, etc. At this point Emma feels calm and quietly confident and has a good night's sleep.

Emma makes sure she has plenty of time to spare before the interview and arrives early. During the interview Emma performs well, but there are a couple of questions she does not know the answers to. At this point Emma's internal dialogue is:
"It's OK. The interviewer doesn't expect me to know everything, as long as I show I have a good overall knowledge of the job."
"What should I say? Just be honest and say you don't know."
Which is exactly what Emma does. The interview ends and Emma knows she has done her best, and she is satisfied with that. Overall an impressive performance.

Alex, like Emma, knows his subject well. The night before, he rehearses the interview material but keeps worrying that maybe he will be asked something he does not know. Alex asks himself:
"What if they ask me something I don't know?"
His inner critic jumps in instantly with:
"Then you'll look stupid and embarrass yourself, and the whole thing will have been a waste of time."
This distracts Alex and makes it hard for him to focus on what he should be doing.

Alex thinks:

"Why am I no good at interviews?"
Again, Alex's inner critic wastes no time in coming back with:
"Because you panic and stumble over your answers, and what's worse is that you put the interviewer off, before you even start, with your sweaty palms."

Then Alex remembers a technique he had been told about, to visualise the interview beforehand. Unfortunately, Alex is not in the best frame of mind and already feels negative about the whole process. So he visualises himself getting more and more anxious as the interview approaches, and he feels this anxiety building up in his body. During the visualisation he thinks:
"What if other more qualified people are going for the role?"
The reply is swift:
"Then they'll get the job, not you."
"What if I can't answer some of the questions?"
"Then you'll go bright red and look like an idiot."
"My hands will be sweaty when I shake the interviewer's hand."

Alex's visualisation of the interview is much more catastrophic since he entered into it with a negative state of mind. Alex spends most of the evening trying to revise for the interview but finds himself constantly distracted by his self-doubt, which makes it difficult to concentrate. He stays up late and does not sleep well, as he anxiously thinks about the interview looming.

On the morning of the interview Alex's thought processes are chaotic, with anxiety coursing through his body. It is hard to concentrate on what he needs to do. As he travels to the interview, in his mind, everything is conspiring against him, especially the traffic. Alex projects his fear and anger onto others in the traffic queues. His anxiety and inner critic have now taken over.

Alex arrives at the interview feeling flustered. He looks around at the other interviewees. He makes assumptions about everyone and builds a story in his head that they are all much better than him. Alex says to himself:
"They all look so professional and relaxed; I must be the least qualified here."

The interview finally arrives, and Alex finds it hard to control the nervous energy. His palms are sweaty when he shakes the interviewer's hand and he focuses on this, which feeds even more into his anxiety. Alex thinks:
"I knew my palms would be sweaty when I shook his hand. What is he going to think of me now?"
"That you're gross, not someone I'd hire. I bet sweat is showing under your armpits now."

The interview starts and Alex composes himself a little. He has a good knowledge of the role and manages to answer some of the questions, but all the while he has an internal dialogue going on.
"Is that the answer he wanted?"
"I bet it's the wrong one, look at his face, he doesn't look impressed."
"Shit, should've given more detail, I bet that's what he wanted."

Alex gets asked another question but now cannot focus sufficiently on the answer because of all the self-doubt coursing through his mind. So he stumbles over the answer and seems unsure of himself.

When asked a question he genuinely does not know the answer to, his mind jumps into overdrive.
"What's the answer?"
"I've no idea, I've messed this all up, there's no way he's going to hire me now."
"I can't just say nothing or say I don't know; I'll look like an idiot."
"I've been quiet too long; I'd better answer quickly."
Alex panics and rambles, rather than saying he does not know. He feels he needs to give an answer and is asking himself:
"Why don't I know this?"
His inner critic is lightning quick in giving a response:
"Because you're an idiot, who doesn't deserve this job."

Alex stumbles through the rest of the interview and is just relieved when it is over. The interviewer has not viewed Alex's performance as negatively as Alex has. He appreciates that Alex has some good experience and handled some of the questions well.

So, what is the message from the interview scenarios above? Although Emma was anxious, she managed to control her anxiety, and visualised a good outcome to the interview, which had a calming effect. Since she then felt more confident, her mind was not as cluttered with internal dialogue. This meant that Emma could concentrate on rehearsing the interview. She also accepted that the interview decision was outside her control, and just concentrated on being her best, rather than trying to second guess the performance and qualifications of other interviewees. This left her mind clear during the interview so that she could focus on her own performance.

Alex however, visualised a negative interview process. He talked himself into being anxious about the material he knew and whether it was enough to get the job. He was worried about other people going for the role and how they may be better qualified than him. Although the other interviewees were outside of Alex's control, he focused a lot of his energy worrying about that. Alex was so focused on his anxiety and his inner critic, that he was not able to prepare himself effectively for the interview.

Alex took every little setback, such as the traffic, personally, as though it was almost a conspiracy against him. Meanwhile his inner critic was stoking the fires of anxiety.

What does anxiety mean?
When you reach a certain level of anxiety, your body goes into 'Fight or Flight' mode. Alex could not run away from the interview - 'Flight' mode (when you sense you are out of danger your body can start to calm down and return to normal), so his body went into 'Fight' mode. In 'Fight or Flight' mode, adrenaline gets pumped into the bloodstream, this then brings about other changes to the body (all unconsciously and rapidly). Your heart rate increases, your breathing becomes more rapid, and glucose is released into your bloodstream, giving rapid energy to all parts of the body. The brain is on high alert. If the perceived threat continues (which it would do in an

> interview situation), then cortisol (the 'stress hormone') is released, keeping the body revved up. Imagine trying to remain calm and composed in an interview situation when all these things are happening internally.

Emma and Alex may be two extreme personalities, one very calm and composed and the other a nervous wreck. However, most of us probably lie somewhere between the two. I hope this illustrates how two different people, both equally qualified, on the same journey, had a very different outcome at the interview. It is how you internalise each situation that matters.

If neither character was successful in getting the role, what do you think their individual responses would be? Think about that for a moment and then we will compare notes.

I believe that Emma would have obviously been disappointed not getting the role, but she knew she had given her best at the interview, and that is all she could ask of herself. She would probably reflect on the interview and be keen to get feedback from the interviewer. I believe she would also believe that whatever the outcome, it was a valuable learning experience which could help improve her future performance.

Alex on the other hand, I believe would be very disappointed not getting the role. He would believe that his interview performance was terrible, even though the interviewer did not view it as negatively as Alex did himself. I think this would feed into Alex's negative narrative about himself; how he cannot get on in his career because he is no good at interviews and all the other interviewees are much better qualified (even though he does not know this as a fact, it is just his belief). Alex would not take constructive criticism well in any feedback, and he only focuses on the negative points. Instead of this being a learning experience, it would just reinforce his view of how he cannot do well at interviews.

In the future when either Emma or Alex go for an interview, their latest experience will be part of the stories they tell themselves about their performance at interviews. When recalling this, it can either be empowering (as in Emma's case) or disempowering (as in Alex's case).

Enough about Emma and Alex. This chapter is called **Your Story** for a reason. What stories are you telling yourself in life, when things do not work out the way you had planned? Are you telling yourself a story before the event, like Alex, where you are setting yourself up to fail?

It is now time to tell your story in the next exercise. It is important to be as honest as you can with yourself. It will not always be easy, but you will benefit the most from this if you are.

Let me give you a couple of examples from my life and the stories I have told myself.

Example 1:
I remember wanting to change my profession from Software Engineer to Personal Performance Coach. I enrolled in the coaching diploma program. The materials sat on my shelf for 10 years before I took action on them.

After 5 years of them sitting there, I told myself that I had left it too long after enrolling (even though the academy offers lifetime learning). I told myself I did not have the time. Yet 10 years later, when I finally started the course, I was busier than ever. At this point I wanted to do it with such a passion, that I made the time.

Example 2:
Another example is when I worked on a contract as a freelance software developer and wanted a raise to my day rate. I remember telling myself that if you ask for this, they may decide they cannot afford to keep you on. I also remember doubting if I was worth it. However, after managing to overcome my self-doubt, I secured the rate rise and went on to work with that client for another couple of years.

In Example 1: I told myself I had left it too long to take action. I was avoiding the commitment by telling myself that. The other thing I told myself was that I did not have the time, yet 10 years later I made the time when I was far busier than I had been. I told myself stories that were not true and they delayed me entering the profession I love. Ultimately, I was avoiding taking action on something by telling myself a story.

In Example 2: I questioned if I was worth the extra rate rise (even though it was modest). I was also worrying that they may think I am too expensive and terminate my contract on that basis. Again, I procrastinated and visualised a bad outcome, which made it a painful and drawn out process, when it was actually a simple question with a pleasing simple answer.

Exercise 1:

Now it is your turn. I want you to dig deep and think of all the stories you tell yourself about your life. Please write them all down with examples. What stories do you tell yourself about the following?
- Why are you not doing the job you love?
- Why have you not started your business yet?
- Why is your business not more successful?
- Why are you not with someone you love?
- Why have you not lost the weight you keep promising yourself you will lose?
- Why do you not own your dream home?

Above are just a few example questions to get you started, but I hope you can think of many more which mean something to you and your current situation

Exercise 2:

I now want you to look at every story you have written down. Think carefully and then answer the following questions:
- Is the story I am telling myself true?
- Where did this story come from?
- Where is the evidence that it is true?
- Is the evidence I have based it on true or just my belief?

To be true, it must be an indisputable fact that someone else would agree on. If it is not, then it is a belief, which is a story you tell yourself to justify not taking action.

A lot of the reasons why we avoid taking action are based on our beliefs rather than fact. We delude ourselves, convincing ourselves it is a fact, when it is actually a belief.

Once we accept that our beliefs are holding us back from action, we can examine our beliefs and get them to start working for us. Having power over our beliefs will help us to tame our inner critic.

Quick Quiz:

Questions
1. What is something that's totally unique about all of us?
2. What type of interview process did Alex visualise?

Answers
1.
2.

The Importance We Attach To Labels

What is a label?

A definition I found in a dictionary was: *a classifying phrase or name applied to a person or thing, especially one that is inaccurate or restrictive.*

I want to talk about labels concerning people and how you use labels to both categorise yourself and others. A label may be only one word, but it can have many attributes.

So what labels have you given to yourself lately? Are you a genius, dunce, average, beautiful, handsome, ugly, short, tall, introvert, extrovert?

Exercise 1:

Write down any labels you use to describe yourself regularly with your self-talk.

What you label yourself as will have a massive impact on the life you lead and the person you perceive yourself to be. Labels are generalisations that you can throw about all the time, some can be empowering and positive, and others can have the opposite effect and be negative and be disempowering.

Labels you give yourself have a much more significant impact than those that are provided to you by society or others. The exception to this would be when you are still young and impressionable. If those that matter to you, such as parents, teachers and friends label you a certain way enough times, you may adopt those labels in your internal dialogue. Again this may not be all bad, as some of these labels may be empowering.

So in exercise 1, you looked at the labels you describe yourself as regularly, in exercise 2, I want you to re-examine those same labels.

Exercise 2:

Review all the labels from exercise 1. Think back to your formative years, were any of these used to describe you by parents, family, teachers or friends?

If in exercise 2, you found that some labels you give yourself are still hanging around since your formative years, are they accurate? I imagine you have changed in so many ways since you were younger. Do these labels you still associate with yourself serve you or act to disempower you?

If you are disempowered, then it is time to cast that old label aside. Remember these are throwaway terms people use to generalise, but when you are young, your brain soaks everything up, and you can take these labels on as part of your identity without realising. Especially if adults dish out these labels, the adults you looked up to at the time.

For instance, I remember having the label 'shy' when I was a child, and even then, I used to hate having that label. As I grew into a teenager, I started pushing back against the label, until I got to the point where I forced myself into uncomfortable social situations (for me at least). After a lot of work on myself, I finally felt free of the label.

Even now, as an ambivert (someone who has a mix of introvert and extrovert characteristics), my default state is introvert, but I can ramp it up like the best of them when I want or need to. Although I had an unhelpful label of being 'shy', I worked on myself to the extent that the label just does not apply anymore. In that respect, I am grateful, as it has served me in a way which made me fight back against it.

What labels are you using to describe yourself that are not serving you, that you can now drop?

> **Exercise 3:**
>
> Looking back to exercise 1, **which labels are not positively serving you?**
>
>
>
> **Which labels would you be happy to let go?**

In exercise 3, you looked at labels that are no longer serving you and some you would now like to let go. How do you go about letting go of labels that you have carried around for a while?

Take the label you no longer want and write it down. Break it up into its constituent parts. From my example earlier, using the 'shy' label, I would break it up like so:

SHY:

Will not approach a stranger to initiate a conversation.

Deflects attention away from themselves.
Feels fear in social situations where they may be asked to contribute publicly in some way.
May think others opinions, ideas and stories are more interesting/important than their own.
Likes to observe conversations rather than fully take part.

So the above are the attributes I would give to the 'shy' label. Remember, you may disagree with my definitions above, and that is fine because labels are subjective and can have different meanings to different people. Use whatever attributes work for you.

Now you have broken it down to what the label means to you, take each descriptive element at a time and find the evidence against it.

So in my case:

I am happy to approach a stranger to initiate a conversation.
I am happy to have the attention on me when I want it to be.
I love to be in social situations.
I like to be a fully contributing member to a conversation.

It is OK not to disprove everything. As above I still have one area I need to focus on, but after disproving the other elements, the 'shy' label no longer fits.

It would serve you well to go through all the labels you give yourself, or others give you and drop the ones that no longer help you.

Just as you can drop labels, you can also adopt labels too. Such as taking traits you already have and then wrapping them in an existing label or making up one of your own. These are your thoughts, in your head, so your rules. Your label can be anything you want it to be.

On a similar point, maybe you would like to have the association of a particular label but do not think you are quite there yet. In that case, take the label and break it down into its attributes and assess yourself against each one. Whatever attributes you feel you are falling short on, work to improve and adapt that new label as your own.

Imagine yourself in an interview situation; you may describe yourself to the interviewer as dependable, responsible, proactive etc. All of these are labels you are attributing to yourself. Your interviewer may ask what does being dependable mean? You then have a chance to describe to the interviewer the attributes that you believe being dependable has. Which then leads to a common understanding of your label. The interviewer may also ask you to give examples of when you have been dependable in the past, to clarify further their knowledge of your interpretation of the label, dependable.

Exercise 4:

How would you describe yourself to other people?

How do you think others would describe you?

Now dig deep and rather than describing yourself to anyone else, **what is your opinion of yourself?**

Are there any differences between the three descriptions above? If there are, why do you think that it is? Are any of the labels you have given yourself other people's labels which you feel you have to conform to, rather than who you genuinely think you are?

We have talked about how labels can impact you, from others labelling you and also from you labelling yourself. How are you labelling others? If you are going to start using labels more healthily for yourself, then it is only right that you give others the same respect.

What labels have you been guilty of giving to others? I am talking about the ones where they are aware you have given them a label (but it does not hurt to be kind in your thoughts too). School children can be some of the worst offenders for this with their playground bullying and taunts. As an adult, even during banter plenty of labels are thrown about, and sometimes if your friend, colleague or family member have a sensitive disposition you are not aware of, they can take these labels to heart which can be upsetting for them. None of us truly knows what is going on in someone else's head or what sensitivities they may have, so first and foremost be kind.

If you are a parent, it is imperative to watch what labels you are using concerning your children. Calling them 'lazy' is a label, and that is lazy speech on your part. I am sure they are not 100% lazy 100% of the time in every situation in their life. They may not have done something you asked them to do, but that is a conversation you could have with them, without calling them lazy. If you try to avoid labelling, you may even find you start having constructive conversations with your teenagers without descending into insulting labels.

Another danger with children is giving them labels which they feel they can not live up to, which adds a lot of pressure to their still-developing minds. Try and start to be more conscious of what you say both to yourself and others and be more specific about what you are saying rather than generalising using a label, which could be misunderstood, as we all have our unique interpretations.

Not only may you not agree on the definition of a label, but you also may not agree on the label itself.

The labels you give to yourself must be empowering and not disempowering. Your inner critic will happily jump in with disempowering labels if you provide it with space, especially if you ask yourself the wrong type of 'Why' questions. Such as: Why can I not lose any weight? Your inner critic will be only too happy to tell you it is because you are 'lazy', 'greedy' etc. Both of these are labels which will not serve you and will just make you feel worse about yourself and your situation.

A better question to circumvent the inner critic would be. What is one small step I could take right now to help me lose weight? Putting the brain into solution mode, rather than inner critic feedback mode, and your mind is genius at finding great solutions for you.

Exercise 5:

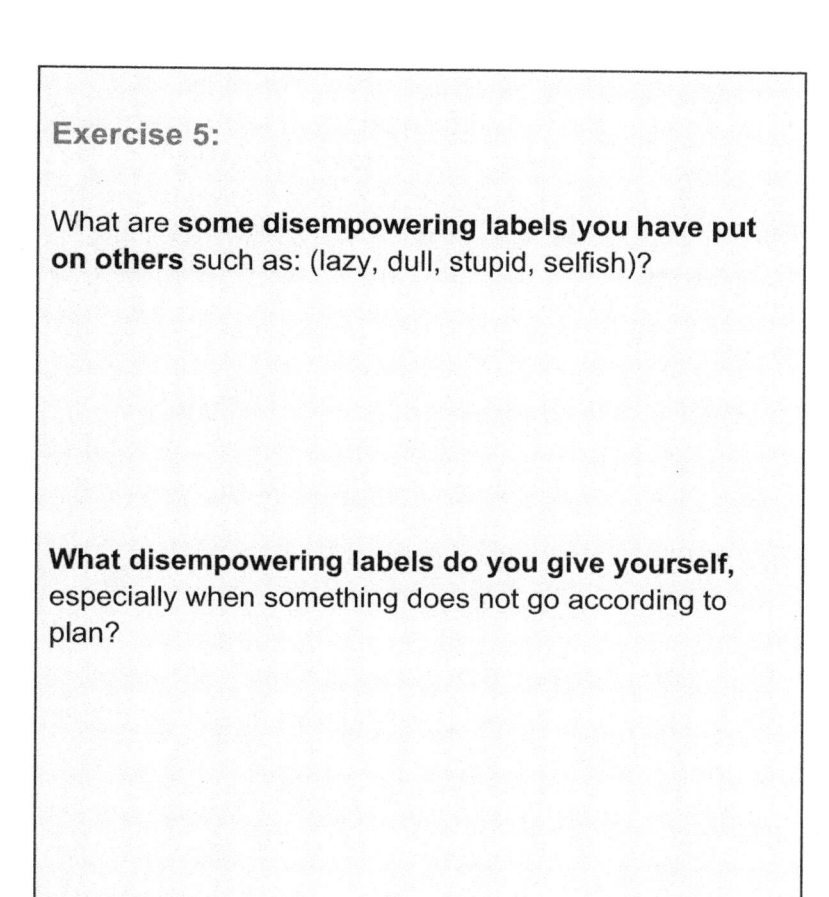

What are **some disempowering labels you have put on others** such as: (lazy, dull, stupid, selfish)?

What disempowering labels do you give yourself, especially when something does not go according to plan?

Reading the above, especially the disempowering labels you have given yourself. How does that make you feel when you read them back? Do you know that when you label someone with a disempowering label, instead of being curious you have just closed off your mind to their potential, and you will then treat them accordingly (including yourself)? Even if you have not specifically called them the label, you will treat them differently (without realising), because you have labelled them in your mind.

However, labels are not all bad news. Yes, they are a generalisation, but they can be positive too if you were to call someone courageous, adventurous, kind, loving. These are all labels which will have different meanings to different people, but they all give off a positive feeling. They are labels to empower rather than to disempower.

Exercise 6:

Write down five positive labels to describe yourself.

Write down five positive labels to describe a loved one.

If you have children, write down five positive labels to describe each child.

Be careful how you label yourself and others as it will have consequences. You can too often casually throw out labels about yourself and others without a second thought.

Labelling yourself in this casual way can seriously limit what you perceive you are capable of doing. Catch yourself when you next throw out a disempowering label in conversation or self-talk and explore it. Is it true what you are saying? Where is the evidence that shows it to be true? Can there be another explanation? Is this label a way you want to describe yourself? How could you be kinder to yourself instead? After all, no one is perfect, and we all have our moments.

Quick Quiz:

Questions
1. Labels you give yourself have a much bigger ......?
2. It is only right when using labels to give others the same ....?
3. Casually labelling yourself can seriously limit what?

Answers
1.
2.
3.

Where Did My Inner Critic Come From?

Your inner critic is part and parcel of your personality. So where did **your** inner critic come from?

In psychology, it is believed that your personality is divided into three parts. These are known as the
- Id
- Ego
- Superego

Let us take these three parts of your personality one at a time to understand how they fit together.

> **Preconscious** - contains everything that can be brought into the conscious mind.
>
> **Conscious** - contains feelings, thoughts and memories that you are currently aware of.
>
> **Unconscious** - contains feelings, thoughts and memories outside of your conscious awareness. It will include things which are unresolved from your past, including pain and anxiety.

The Id

This is the only part of your personality that you are born with. You hear a baby screaming and crying because she is hungry or uncomfortable, you are dealing with the Id. If you are holding the hand of a toddler having a temper tantrum and throwing himself on the supermarket floor, that is the Id.

The Id is the first part of your personality and resides entirely in your unconscious mind (outside of your awareness), it is known as the biological component and has no concept of the real world outside. The Id is responsible for your primal and instinctive urges, such as hunger, aggression and sex. It has no concept of the needs of others and is solely focused on what you need or want at any particular time.

Apart from the attributes already mentioned, the Id is also selfish, illogical and chaotic. It does not matter what thoughts or experiences you have in life, none of these will influence the Id. It has no thought processes, never matures and continues to be driven by desire throughout your life. The Id is governed by what is known as the **pleasure principle**.

> **Pleasure Principle** (pleasure-pain principle) – This is the driving force of the Id. It seeks to gratify your basic needs immediately (hunger, thirst, anger and sex), without any regard to the consequences.

The Id is by no means the villain though. It is there to ensure that your most basic needs are met, which may mean the difference between life and death. The Id is also the powerhouse of your personality and driving force behind it.

The Ego

Next up in personality development is the Ego, which is thought to develop between the ages of two and three. The Ego develops from the Id and ensures the Id's desires can be expressed in socially acceptable ways in the real world.

Whereas the Id strictly resides in the unconscious, the Ego functions in the unconscious, preconscious and conscious mind. The Ego is the part of your personality which deals with reality, it is the part we all identify with and know best. It is what we would call our conscious mind. The Ego functions based on the **reality principle**.

> **Reality Principle** – This helps you consider the risks and the possible outcomes when you are making a decision. The Id wants a drink, but unfortunately, you are in a meeting and cannot have one now. Leave it to the Id and you would be jumping across the table and grabbing your boss's bottle of water and guzzling it down. However, the Ego intervenes with the reality principle and ensures the Id's urges are met when it is suitable and appropriate.

A prime part of the Ego's function is to regulate the Id, and aim to satisfy its demands in a much more realistic and socially acceptable way. Often it is not appropriate for an impulse to be satisfied immediately, so the Ego will seek to delay gratification until it is a suitable time and place.

Imagine being in a meeting at work and there is still 30 minutes remaining. You suddenly get the hunger impulse (Id) and it is a craving for something sweet. To keep the Id satisfied the Ego will conjure up an image from the real world using a mechanism called **secondary process thinking**.

> **Secondary Process Thinking** - This is where the Ego matches an Id's visualisation of what it wants with a real-world object to dissipate the Id's energy. So, for example, the Id craves something sweet, and the urge cannot be met immediately, secondary process thinking intervenes and you fantasise about eating a chocolate bar until that urge can be satisfied.

The Id has been compared to a horse and the Ego to the rider. Without a rider, the horse can do what it wants, where it wants, whenever it wants. A horse with a rider can be reined in and guided.

The Superego

The Superego is the last part of a personality to develop. It is thought to develop between the ages of three to five years. The Superego is effectively your sense of what is right or wrong. Like the Ego, the Superego functions in the conscious, preconscious and unconscious parts of the mind.

The Superego contains your morals and ideals. These are acquired over time from your parents and anyone else who has an influence in your life, such as society at large. In terms of the Superego, it aims to repress the Id's urges (especially ones forbidden by society such as aggression) and get the Ego to behave idealistically rather than realistically.

The Superego is divided into two systems:
1. **Ideal self**: - the Superego has an ideal of what it believes the Ego should live up to and includes rules and behaviours the Ego should follow.
2. **Conscience**: - holds ideas about things that parents and society may view as bad. Acting on these behaviours could lead to bad consequences, punishment or feelings of guilt.

The Superego holds this idea of an ideal self, and if you do not live up to this image, you may be punished by feelings of guilt. When you do live up to the image, you may experience feelings of pride. If the ideal self is unattainable, then whatever you do will be perceived as a failure.

How the Id, Ego and Superego Interact

This is all about how your brain behaves rather than distinct physical parts of the brain. Your distinct personality is the culmination of the Id, Ego and Superego working together.

From a high level, the Id will make demands, the Ego will look to satisfy those demands in a realistic way and the Superego will add its ideals and morality.

It is the Ego that mediates between the demands of the Id and the ideals and morals of the Superego and tries to reconcile these in a realistic way.

A healthy personality is where there is a balance between the Id, Ego and Superego.

Someone with a dominant Id may be impulsive and end up as a criminal because they act on their most basic urges.

A dominant Superego may lead someone to become very judgemental.

You and Your Inner Critic

So, have you guessed which of the Id, Ego or Superego is responsible for your inner critic?

Drum roll, please. Your inner critic is, in fact, your **Superego**.

Most, if not all of us, have an inner critic. For some, it may only be a whisper, but for others, it can be all-consuming and overwhelming. For the majority, the inner critic will be an anchor that weighs down on your dreams and holds you back from daring to realise them.

In images, the Id is often portrayed as the devil with its primitive needs, wants and instant gratification. But in reality, it is an essential part of who you are and aids in your survival. The Ego is often pictured as the regular person, as it is your Ego which you most closely identify with in your personality. The Superego is commonly displayed as an angel, the idea being that your Superego constrains your Id and gets you to aspire to greater things.

However, as you know, the Superego is no angel and can feel demonic at times when being a full-on inner critic. However, just as the Id is an essential part of your personality and is there to ensure your survival, the Superego is also playing its part in keeping you 'safe'.

The Superego is trying to ensure that your Id does not get what it wants if it contravenes society's laws or morals. The Superego has built up another database of rights and wrongs which it has collated from your parents and other influential people in your life, from childhood to your teenage years. This is based around punishments and approvals you received, mainly from your parents, but others too. When you break your Superego's rules it produces feelings of guilt or anxiety.

Let us look at two examples of how a Superego rule may form in childhood.

Example 1:
As a child, you strike out and hit another child (driven by your Id). Your parents catch you doing this, and you are scolded. This then leads you to realise that being aggressive is unacceptable. This rule will be stored for reference and will affect your future behaviour. This is an example of a good healthy Superego rule which serves you and society.

Example 2:
As a child, you are in a classroom situation and you put your hand up to answer a question. You get the answer

wrong, are berated by the insensitive teacher and your fellow classmates laugh at you. To protect yourself from future feelings of anxiety and embarrassment, your Superego steps in and creates a new rule, that you must avoid volunteering to give your view to others. Unfortunately, this is an unhealthy rule which could affect your future by not having confidence in your own opinions and feeling they are not valued by others.

To move from theory to reality, here are some examples from my personal experience, which are based on when I was at high school, and how they affected my future behaviour.

Personal Example 1:
In an English lesson in high school, we were taught how to write poetry that does not rhyme (free verse). We were asked to write a poem from our imagination. My poem was about a duck breaking the ice in a pond on a winter's day. We handed the poems in and when the teacher read mine, she absolutely loved it, asked me to read it out in front of the class and it was published in the school magazine. My new stored rule was that you can do no wrong with free verse poetry, you are a genius, and everybody loves it. I was envisioning my future career as a poet. Wow, I had arrived, and I was a rock star at poetry.

Personal Example 2:
A substitute English teacher was taking our class on this day. He was talking about poetry, but this time, the more traditional rhyming form. He set us an exercise to write a rhyming poem and then hand it in. I still had my reference from last time where I remembered all the pleasure and positive feedback I had received. I was a rock star poet and so it was time to show off my prowess once again. Because I was so good, I could ignore the brief and impress him with an artistic poem that did not rhyme. I crafted my verse and handed my work in, along with everyone else. I was waiting for my spot in the limelight again. I did not have to wait long. He got to my poem, rightly pointed out that I had not written in rhyme, and berated me in front of the whole class, telling me that I must be stupid. I sank down in my chair, turned beetroot red, and felt the eyes of my classmates upon me. The new rule was to overwrite the old rule and never write poetry again.

With personal example 1, I had let my Superego get carried away, creating a rule which led me to believe that I could do no wrong, even to the point of ignoring a teacher's instructions. That rule was unhealthy and did not serve me well or for long.

In personal example 2, after my dressing down from the teacher, there was an overcorrection to my rule. The new rule was to avoid writing poetry or if you must do it, be purposefully mediocre so you do not get noticed or picked out. Again, an overreaction and an unhealthy rule. Somewhere between the two extreme rules would have been great, but no one can accuse your Superego of being logical.

Personal Example 3:
Let's finish with an example that has a happy ending. This is also set in high school, during physical education with a new teacher. I was not a keen runner and hated long-distance running. He was one of those teachers who just knew exactly what to do and say to inspire you. He would single you out and build you up in front of everybody, so you felt a million dollars and like anything was possible.

We were running 100-metre sprints out on the track, as well as 400 metres and 800 metres. He was really encouraging outside, but it was when we returned to the classroom that he landed the killer comment. He singled me out (probably knew that I needed a boost of self-belief) and said in front of everyone, that Mike had sprinted 100 metres today and was only 3 seconds off the world record. Right then and there, my mind was blown. Wow, I'm nearly at a world record pace, I thought to myself, not knowing that 3 seconds is an eternity in a 100-metre sprint.

However, the comments had done their magic and I was now a runner and loved it. It is amazing how your mindset can change in an instant. Since then I have run many half-marathons and even managed the London marathon once. I see that as a very healthy rule brought about by an amazing teacher.

I hope you can relate to the examples above, where you create a rule, which may later be abandoned and replaced with a new rule. Some of these rules may be healthy and others not so much.

It is the unhealthy rules/beliefs you create which allow the inner critic to have a voice. This voice comes when you start thinking about breaking the rule, moving out of your comfort zone and challenging yourself.

Exercise 1:

As with the previous examples, I would like you to think back to your past. Anything from childhood up until your late teens, and write down one example of something you did, which got a reaction you did not like.

How did that make you feel at the time?

What has that stopped you doing as an adult?

Now come back to the present time and think of that same incident. **What would you say as a caring adult to yourself as a child?**

It may have been a healthy reprimand; in which case the rule is good. However, if it isn't a good rule that is serving you well, then **rewrite it to what you now think it should be, and abandon the old rule**.

Exercise 2:

Now think back to a time you were praised or rewarded for doing something in the past and **write down how that made you feel.**

What positive benefits has this had on your life and encouraged you to do or try as an adult?

Quick Quiz:

Questions
1. What three parts is your personality divided into?
2. What part of your personality does the pleasure principle belong to?
3. What two systems is the superego divided into?

Answers
1.
2.
3.

Imposter Syndrome

Ever felt like you do not belong and that at any moment your colleagues or friends will find you out and realise you are a fraud? You may look at other colleagues and judge them as confident in what they do, and you feel like you are battling to keep your head above water.

Commonly known as Imposter Syndrome, and it is estimated to affect as many as 70% of people at some point in their lives.

Do you believe you have got to where you are just by luck rather than by the skills you have? Then you are suffering from imposter syndrome.

I know from personal experience what this is like, and it is a distressing and stressful experience. Always worrying, you will be 'found out' at any moment.

I have been a freelance contractor in the I.T. industry for 22 years, and during that whole time, I was waiting to get 'found out'. Contractors that don't make the grade usually get dumped pretty quickly with potentially a week or even just a days notice. I had been in some contracts for up to 3 years, having had my contract renewed multiple times. Yet still, I felt at any moment; they would realise I was not good enough and that I had just been lucky so far.

I was always self-critical, and at times when I did not have an adequate understanding of something I did not always ask for it to be clarified. Thinking about it rationally, it makes perfect sense, if you don't understand something, then get clarification. But to me asking those questions, meant showing everyone I did not know what I was doing and therefore was not up to the job.

Looking at this now, in the cold light of day, I can see I was misguided, but at the time it was all too real and stressful. When you read the types of imposter syndromes there are; you will realise I was a soloist. But at the time, I did not feel I had imposter syndrome; instead, I just believed I **was** the imposter and had to do my best not to get 'found out'.

If when you are reading any of the descriptions listed, and you recognise yourself and feel that you do suffer from imposter syndrome, then take a step back and try to gather evidence of how you got to where you are. I can tell you categorically that no one in my profession gets there by luck and I am sure that is the same for most other jobs too.

There are five types of Imposter Syndrome, according to Dr Valerie Young, who is a recognised expert on Imposter Syndrome :

The Perfectionist:

The perfectionist will always look to attain near-perfect results, which in the real world are hard to achieve and is setting the perfectionist up for potential failure before they have even begun. A perfectionist will rarely be satisfied with what they have done as they will always feel they could have done better. Their focus will be on anything that did not go as planned rather than all the great work they achieved.

How do you know if you are a perfectionist? Ask yourself these questions.
- Are you resistant to delegating your work?
- Should all your work be perfect, all of the time?
- If you do not hit your perfect target, do you chastise yourself and dwell on it for days on end?
- Has anyone ever told you that you are a micromanager?

How can you mitigate being a perfectionist?
- Celebrate the wins along the way and what went well.
- Remember 'Done' is better than 'Perfect', so make an early start even before you think you are ready.
- Accept that it will never be perfect, but each imperfection is a learning experience you can use to improve for next time.

The Superman / Superwoman:

The Superman or Superwoman pushes themselves and works harder than anyone else on the team to prove they are not an imposter. These people need to succeed in all areas of life and feel like they are continually accomplishing something. Convinced they are frauds in amongst all the 'genuinely' skilled people that they work with daily.

How do you know if you are a Superman / Superwoman? Ask yourself these questions.
- Are you always the last one in the office or the last at signing off the system at night if working from home?

- Do you feel the need to continually prove your worth, despite having all the necessary qualifications?
- Are hobbies now just a distant memory, because of the amount of time you feel you need to dedicate to your work?
- Does it feel stressful having some relaxation or downtime from work and you view it as wasting your time, that you could use to work instead?

How can you mitigate being a superman/superwoman?
- Do not take constructive criticism personally, but look at it as a chance to learn.
- Try to work on your self-worth believing you are good enough, rather than waiting for external validation from your boss or colleagues.
- Work on accepting you are good enough and qualified enough to do the job in hand and gradually ease off on the workload.

The Natural Genius:

The Natural Genius is someone who usually does not have to try too hard as skills come naturally to them. When something takes a lot more effort, and they have to work harder at it than usual, they start to believe they are an imposter.

How do you know if you are a Natural Genius? Ask yourself these questions.
- Do you avoid doing things you are not good at because it makes you feel uncomfortable?

- Do you feel like you can handle everything on your own and do not need a mentor to help guide you?
- Are you used to not putting much effort in, but still produce great results?
- Does your confidence fail if things take longer or do not work out as planned?
- When you were a child, did you get told how smart you are?

How can you mitigate being a natural genius?
- Do not put off things you are not good at, instead embrace the learning challenge.
- Although you are used to being naturally good at some things, explore outside your comfort zone and build other skills over time, to make you a more rounded person.
- Look at yourself as someone who will learn and grow lifelong.

The Soloist:

The Soloist, feels they have to achieve things on their own and if they have to ask for help, then they are an imposter.

How do you know if you are a Soloist? Ask yourself these questions.
- When you ask for assistance, do you relate it to the project requirements rather than your own needs?
- Do you feel the need to achieve things on your own, without asking for help?
- I can do this on my own. Sound familiar?

How can you mitigate being a soloist?

- By not asking for help when you need it, you could be slowing down the whole team's project. Colleagues and your boss would much rather you ask for help when you need it, as it is a team effort and that means working fully as part of a team and not on your own.
- Ask for help early rather than waiting, better little and often, than waiting until things become harder to resolve and deadlines loom.

The Expert:

The Expert needs to know all the fine detail of a project before even beginning it. They like to get as many qualifications and certifications as possible to improve their skills. They fear not knowing enough and being 'found out' as an imposter, so continually strive to improve their skillset.

How do you know if you're an Expert? Ask yourself these questions.
- Will, you only apply for jobs where you meet all the criteria?
- Are you hesitant to ask questions in a group or speak up in meetings in case you do not know the answer?
- Do you fear when someone calls you an expert?
- Even if you have been in your job for a long time and are in a senior position, do you still feel like you do not know enough?

How can you mitigate being an expert?

- When you are worried about not knowing the answer in a meeting or group, the chances are others will not know the answer either. As well as getting a better understanding yourself, you will also be helping colleagues gain a better understanding too. So ask that question.
- Why not apply for the job where you meet 60% or more of the criteria. The worst that can happen is you will not get the job, so no worse than if you had not applied in the first place, plus you will gain valuable experience through the application process.

So what does this all have to do with your inner critic? Well, imposter syndrome is all down to the self-talk you are carrying on in your head, and if you ask a terrible question, you know your inner critic will be all over it in a flash.

So if you find yourself suffering from imposter syndrome, then try and identify what your imposter type is and then follow the mitigation strategies listed.

As well as that, it would be good if you can share how you feel with others to understand that what you are thinking and feeling is not based on reality.

Take small steps and build on them, not looking for perfection, but incremental learning.

Do not compare yourself to others as we all excel at different things, and we are all on our journeys. Try to embrace your journey and not compare it to anyone else's.

Exercise 1:

Be honest with yourself and look at all the things over the last year you either feel you have done well or others have remarked you have done an excellent job. **Now list these down**. Starting the recording of your evidence that you are not an imposter.

As time goes on, every time something goes well (no matter how small) or someone comments positively on your work, write it down and thank them. Building up your growing body of evidence that you are great at what you do. You may doubt yourself, but look at the evidence and see yourself in a different light.

In the example, I gave of myself earlier, where I was feeling imposter syndrome as a soloist. Part of the mitigation strategy is to ask questions first, rather than wait until you have to. As otherwise you will be potentially putting a project deadline in peril, especially if someone else is waiting on your work to be complete on time.

It was a real battle with myself, to ask questions early and try and be more curious as I felt asking those questions would reveal my weakness, and I would be 'found out'. All the time, however, my real fault was not asking those questions early and dragging my feet. I just could not see it at the time. In the end, I realised I had to act, and although it felt uncomfortable at least initially, over time, it led to better productivity on my part as well as less stress.

Exercise 2:

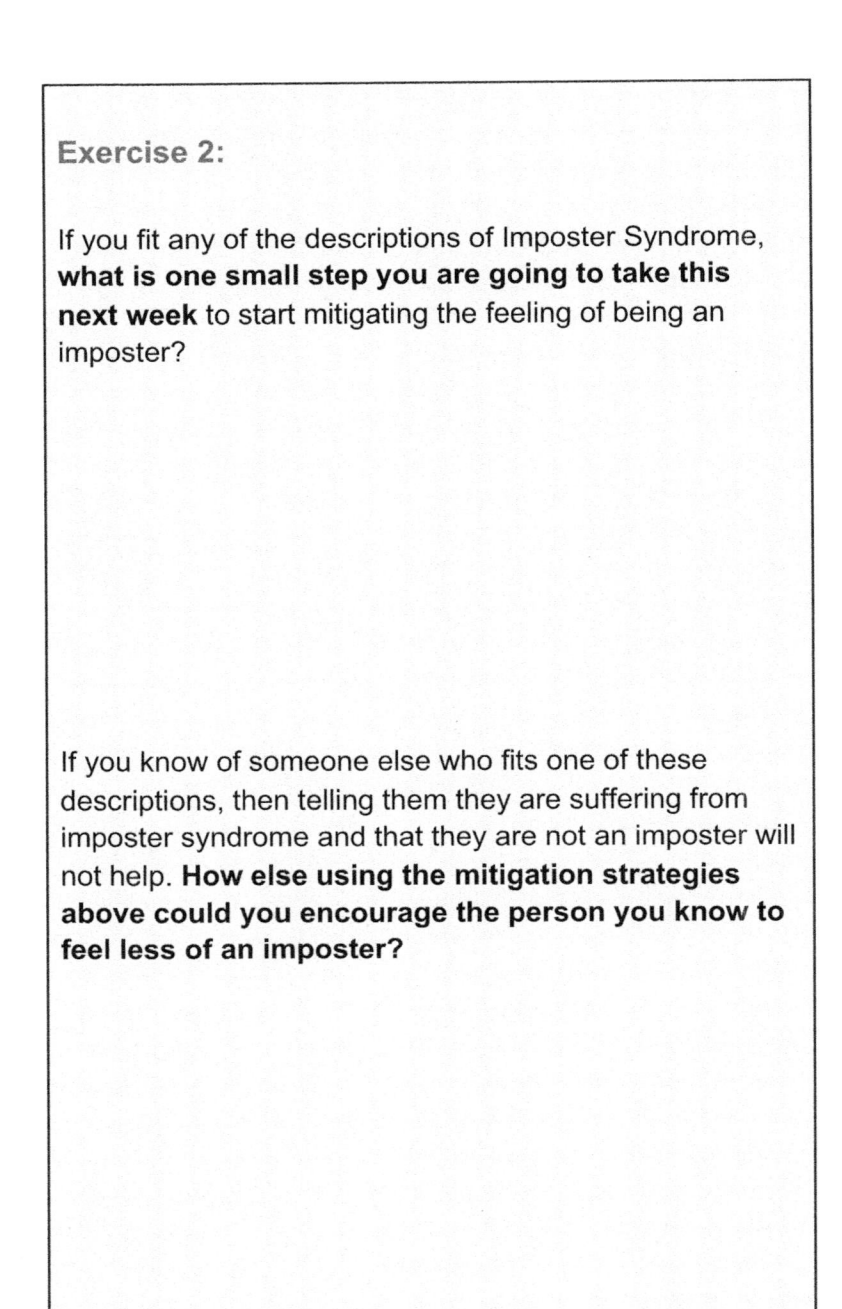

If you fit any of the descriptions of Imposter Syndrome, **what is one small step you are going to take this next week** to start mitigating the feeling of being an imposter?

If you know of someone else who fits one of these descriptions, then telling them they are suffering from imposter syndrome and that they are not an imposter will not help. **How else using the mitigation strategies above could you encourage the person you know to feel less of an imposter?**

Quick Quiz:

Questions
1. Who is the recognised expert on Imposter Syndrome?
2. What type of Imposter Syndrome does not have to try too hard as skills come naturally to them?
3. Who should you not compare yourself to?

Answers
1.
2.
3.

Listening In On Your Inner Critic

Let me begin this chapter by stating that having negative thoughts is entirely normal and part of the human experience. You have a lot of thoughts on a typical day, being in the thousands. A lot of these will most likely be in your subconscious, and you will not even be aware of them.

Also, a fair portion of these thoughts will be negative, again, that makes you an entirely regular member of the human race. It only becomes a problem when you start to dwell on those negative thoughts and give them energy by believing in them.

In this chapter, I will be asking you to look at and spend time analysing your negative thoughts. However, spending time in this way will not be giving these thoughts more power; the opposite is true; you will be looking at these thoughts rather than buying into them. Empowering you to challenge, rather than accept these thoughts.

My inner critic has been my constant companion throughout my life or as far back as I can remember. Telling me, I was not good enough or not capable of doing countless things during my life. I am so relieved I have used the strategies throughout this book, and now my inner critic is a shadow of its former self.

That is not to say it has disappeared altogether and just in case you are wondering, that will not happen. In this book I am not trying to teach you how to get rid of your inner critic once and for all, as I believe that is not possible, but rather, as the title of the book says to tame your inner critic. Take the inner critic's power away and put you back in the driving seat.

I have my inner critic under control, especially when I have the chance to step back and assess what is going on objectively. However, there are still times when my inner critic surfaces and catches me off guard. For example, I was doing a presentation the other day to just over 50 people. Something distracted me for a second, and then my inner critic was in there as quick as a shot. Telling me that you have lost your train of thought, now you are going to make a mess of the presentation. As I switched between browser tabs I got confused for a moment; I thought to myself, take a deep breath, it is okay. What seems like an eternity to me as a presenter, is only a second or two for the audience.

My primary defence against these inner critic moments is to prepare well beforehand. In this instance, I had prepared well, so as soon as I lost my footing in the presentation, I quickly referred to my notes (my safety net) and carried on from where I had left off, with my audience none the wiser.

In a previous chapter, you were discovering your story and writing down your examples. Where did those thoughts originate?

Is there a voice in your mind you are used to hearing?

A voice that prevents you from leaving your comfort zone and taking a risk or trying something new.

A voice that tells you I am not good enough, I will fail if I try, it is not worth taking the risk, it could be embarrassing, what will people think about me?

The next exercise is about catching yourself when you have a thought that is critical of you or when you are starting to doubt yourself.

Listen in to that doubting voice and start to tell it apart from your other thoughts, which are not judgmental.

Exercise 1:

Are there some common phrases that come up for you time after time from your inner critic?

If you are not somewhere you can quickly write things down, and you have an inner critic moment, maybe you could capture it in your phone notes or similar.

This exercise is much harder than it initially sounds. You are so used to hearing your inner critic as part of your everyday thoughts; you just accept them without question—time to concentrate and listen deeply.

If you can capture the inner critic moments as they happen and write them down, then at the end of the day, you can look at how you talk to yourself. It is crucial as when you do this; you start to realise how often your inner critic pops up to disrupt your thoughts.

What inner critic thoughts have you had today?

After doing exercise 1, what did you find out? Do you have many more critical thoughts in a day than you realised?

If you did not manage to find many, then that is fantastic news as it may mean you already have your inner critic under control or maybe you need to revisit the exercise and focus even more.

Look for things where you are going to do something and then decide you will not do it after all. What was it that made you change your mind? Could it be that your inner critic has shown up with a doubting voice?

Also notice when you either feel fearful about a situation or your emotions dip. Think, what is the reason for this fear or the change in my emotions. Were there some inner critic thoughts coming up, getting you to doubt your abilities?

> **Exercise 2:**
>
> I want you now to revisit the list of critical thoughts you had in exercise 1. **Read every thought out loud and then think to yourself, would I say these things to anyone else?**
>
> **How would you feel if your best friend talked to you like that?** Would they be your best friend for long?

After completing exercise 2, I hope you realise you deserve better and you deserve to be more compassionate with yourself. If you would not let a best friend talk to you like that and you would not treat others like that, then why on earth, would you treat yourself like this through listening to your inner critic?

It is time to start taking more control of the critical thoughts you are having.

Exercise 3:

In the previous exercises, you have noted your critical thoughts down and reviewed how your inner critic voice talks to you.

Now go through each of your inner critic's thoughts and phrases from exercise 1. **Replace what is there with what a supportive friend would say instead.** If you find this too challenging to do on your own, maybe you could ask a supportive friend what they would say to each of your inner critic's thoughts.

How do you feel after exercise 3? Hopefully, you can see how being more compassionate with yourself leads to a feeling of well being.

Remember, your inner critic wants to keep you in your comfort zone. If you do not try, then the result is always a failure. To grow, you need to move beyond your comfort zone.

A quote I love is:

Your comfort zone is a wonderful place, but nothing ever grows there.

Every time you have a negative thought brought about by your inner critic, remember that if you accept that thought, your self-confidence and self-esteem may be affected. Think of how you would talk to someone else. If you would not speak to anyone else like that, then give yourself that same respect too.

The critical thing to realise is; do not try and control your thoughts. Sure you can control what you think for a few minutes, but before you know it, your thoughts have drifted into something else entirely of their own accord.

Trying to control what you think is an exhausting task; it is why I don't believe positive thinking is a productive long-term strategy. There is nothing inherently wrong in trying to think positive, but you have to make an effort to do that. As soon as you get distracted, your mind will go off on its journey of thoughts once again, so it will be a never-ending battle.

When you have listened in to your inner critic, it is not about controlling the thoughts; it is about acknowledging, they are only thoughts. Thoughts are not facts, they are simply made up in our mind, and so you have the power to observe the thought and then let it go. You do not need to act or focus on it.

However, at times, no matter how hard you try, you can not escape from your inner critic with its negative self-talk. In this case, stop thinking altogether and use a distraction technique, such as doing something, which will take your focus away from critical thinking and essentially give your mind a chance to reset itself.

One thing you can instantly do wherever you are, and no matter your situation is to focus on your breathing. Changing your breathing can immediately change your state as well as being a great distraction technique. This technique is called the **4 7 8 breathing technique**. Do the following:
- Close your mouth and inhale quietly through your nose for the count of 4.
- Hold your breath for a count of 7.
- Exhale through your mouth to the count of 8. (if you want to embrace this, then make a whoosh sound as you are exhaling).

One other strategy to try if you are struggling to get your inner critic to quiet down is to write down what your inner critic says. Acknowledge it, then tell your inner critic that this does not serve or help you, so you are going to let this negativity go. Then either throw it away or burn it (if safe to do so). Letting go in this way can be a cathartic process to carry out, and you may even enjoy it.

So far, you have looked at the negative thoughts that flow through your mind, noted them down and then re-interpreted them as a compassionate close friend. Over time and with practice, this will allow you to catch a negative thought and just let it drift by knowing that it is a harsh and unrealistic judgement of yourself and has no basis in reality.

I would like to end this chapter with a metaphor called the bubble machine.

It is an excellent metaphor for those with busy minds and those who suffer from anxiety.

Imagine a children's bubble machine. One that plugs into the wall, so it runs continuously. You fill it with a bubble mixture, and it has a wheel which rotates around continuously. On this wheel, there are lots of little arms, each with a round hoop at the end. As it spins it gets dipped into the bubble mixture and then when it reaches the top of the wheel, it passes over a small jet of air, which blows on the hoop, pushing into the bubble mixture and forms a bubble which floats off.

Now think of your mind as the bubble machine. It is continuously switched on and working. Think of the bubbles as your thoughts. Every time a thought is created, it drifts in your mind like a bubble in the air, and just like a bubble, a thought is transient, meaning it will pass. The bubble ultimately pops and disappears, and you can think of your thoughts in the same way, as disappearing or even popping.

Every thought is transient; it will pass; thoughts are never permanent. You do not have to do anything, just let it pass, and it will 'pop' and disappear of its own accord.

However, sometimes, in your mind, you latch onto a negative or troubling thought. It is like the bubble machine, with the wheel getting stuck at the top. The air blows in, making the bubble bigger and bigger as more air fills the bubble.

Just like when you focus on a negative thought and think about it and dwell on it, you give it more power and make it bigger and bigger, just like the stuck bubble.

Instead, you have the choice of letting go of the thought, so this too will then pass of its own accord. All you have to know is if you let the thought drift by, without acting on it, without focussing on it, it will pass.

Quick Quiz:

Questions
1. Where does nothing ever grow?
2. What is the breathing technique called that can help change your state and distract your mind?
3. Thoughts are never permanent; they are ………?

Answers
1.
2.
3.

Taming Your Inner Critic

If you have not already, it is time to give your inner critic a name. For example, mine is called the Trogg (but that is a whole other story). It has got to be something meaningful to you, and why not have some fun with it?

Exercise 1:

What name are you going to give your inner critic?

My inner critic's name is:

There could be potentially many different ways of taming your inner critic, and in this book, along with all the other strategies introduced so far, you will look at a further two techniques that I have found worked for my clients and myself in the past.

Acknowledge your Inner Critic

Some people find that the mere acknowledgement of their inner critic is enough to feel at ease. It is accepting you have an inner critic and in this scenario, you are accepting and thanking them for trying to protect you.

Your inner critic started forming in childhood, and it remains in that childlike state, and you can not reason with it. Your inner critic is protecting you from what a child may have perceived as dangerous because of parental or others influence. But now you have grown and certainly outgrown your inner critic.

Your inner critic perceives moving out of your comfort zone and into the unknown as potentially harmful and dangerous. In ancient times this could have been the case. However, in the modern world, despite its imperfections, you are safer than ever.

So thank your inner critic for having your back and looking out for you. Be patient and kind and realise when you are talking to your inner critic, you are talking to a small frightened child. The more outside your comfort zone you want to go, for example, taking on a big project which involved a lot of risks or unknowns, the louder your inner critic may get. Again, imagine a frightened child.

So in this instance, you thank your inner critic, whatever you have called it and say it is OK. I have outgrown you, and I am the adult in this relationship, so step back, trust me and let me get on with what I need to do.

In this technique, you hear, acknowledge, thank and then take back control and tell your inner critic you are the adult and in the driving seat, and there is no need to worry.

Clients have found doing this, when the inner critic voice starts, calms their mind so they can carry on with the task in hand.

Reframing your Inner Critic

A different way of dealing with your inner critic is using the reframing technique. This technique is useful if either the first one does not work or if you find your inner critic, particularly obstructive.

You are going to look at a technique called reframing, adapted from NLP (Neuro-Linguistic Programming). Reframing uses both your visual and auditory senses within your imagination to recreate your inner critic in a form much easier to brush aside and ignore.

The idea is to take away the power your inner critic has over you and put you firmly back in charge and back in the driving seat.

As with all the exercises, within this book, it is only by fully taking part, that you can start to make that change. Just reading the book and intellectualising it, will not bring about change, you have to fully immerse yourself within the exercise to get the most benefit.

Exercise 2:

You must see your inner critic as separate from yourself and your other non-judgemental thoughts. Part one of that was to name it. Now I want you to listen to their voice, how does it sound?
- Is it masculine or feminine?
- Does it have an accent?
- Is it a deep voice or not?
- How quickly does it speak?

Write down the characteristics of your inner critic's voice in as much detail as possible.

When you have described your inner critic's voice in detail, how does it make you feel?

In exercise 2, you imagined the voice your inner critic uses when it talks to you. It is essential to think in detail just how your inner critic sounds. Does it speak in a fast, aggressive manner or sarcastically? The more detail you can build up in your mind, the better.

The next exercise takes the voice you described in exercise 2 and transforms it in exercise 3.

Important Note: exercise 3 onwards may be something outside of your comfort zone (and we know who wants to keep you there). To get the maximum benefit, please complete them as described and fully immerse yourself in the experience.

Exercise 3:

Conjure up your inner critic's voice one more time.

Now you are going to change it.

I want you to imagine a voice that would make you laugh instead of cringe. An excellent way to do this is to imagine your inner critic talking to you and then start to speed up the voice until it makes you smile. Now make it sound squeaky, like a cartoon character.

At this point just for fun, you could add a funny accent that makes you smile.

Now imagine the voice getting further and further away, so the volume level goes right down.

At this point, you should have a squeaky, sped-up voice, with a possibly funny accent and its volume is drifting lower as it sounds further and further away.

How ridiculous does this new voice sound? Describe the unique voice you have given your inner critic in detail to embed every nuance of it within your mind. Then you can instantly recall it next time your inner critic starts talking and transform the voice into the one you've chosen.

Now you have changed your inner critic's voice, describe how the new voice makes you feel?

In exercise 3, you have started to reclaim your power and loosen the hold your inner critic has on you.

In this next exercise, you are going to visualise your inner critic in detail and then recreate them in the image you choose, to disempower the voice of your inner critic further.

Up until now, you may have just had a vague idea of how your inner critic looks. Your inner critic may be based on a person/animal in the real world. In the next exercise, it is time to go into detail.

Exercise 4:

If you are a visual person and you visualise your inner critic, then this next step will suit you. I want you to imagine your inner critic, in as much detail as possible. Think of everything.

- Are they human, some people see their inner critic as an animal?
- If your inner critic takes human form, answer the questions below, if not, describe what you see instead in as much detail as you can.
  - How tall are they?
  - Their hair, what colour, long or short, what style?
  - Their face and its features, what colour are their eyes, how big is their nose, ears & chin?
  - What are they wearing? Describe it in detail.
  - How do they hold themselves? How is their posture?

Write down how your inner critic looks in detail.

After describing your inner critic in detail, how does it make you feel?

Now you should have a complete and detailed image of your inner critic. It is time to have some fun. Just like you did with your inner critic's voice earlier, you are now going to transform your inner critic's image. You are effectively giving your inner critic a makeover.

In the next exercise, you will be disempowering your inner critic's hold over you.

Exercise 5:

Now, I want you to do the following:
- Visualise your inner critic. Now watch them as they start slowly shrinking down in size. How small do you want them to be? I have shrunk my inner critic down to be as small as my thumb.
- You have seen the caricature artists on holiday, now visualise how you could make your inner critic a caricature. How would they look? You could even turn them into a cartoon version of themselves if you like. Imagine them in a ridiculous pose. Change their hair to look silly or get rid of it altogether, Visualise every detail.
- Now take out all of the colours from your visualisation of your inner critic and make the visualisation a bit grainy, like old film footage, so your inner critic looks like a character from an old black and white movie.
- If your inner critic is moving, then perhaps you could imagine them moving very quickly or very slowly, whichever makes you feel best.

Having changed your visualisation of your inner critic, how do you feel now?

At this point, your inner critic should be tiny compared to how you visualised them before. They may look like a cartoon version of themselves or a caricature with exaggerated features. Your visualisation should be a grainy black and white image. Picture your inner critic in detail and see how small and insignificant they look compared to you.

Remember the voice exercise you carried out on your inner critic earlier? Now it is time to bring that into play too. You have your grainy black & white, small image of your cartoon-like inner critic talking to you in the voice you imagined for them earlier.

Exercise 6:

Repeat this exercise at least six times to embed the feeling of your new representation of your inner critic. Believe in the process if you want this to be as effective as possible.

As you have the small grainy image of your inner critic in your mind and have also got them talking in their ridiculous voice, **I want you to think how that makes you feel about your inner critic.**

It is vital to capture this new feeling in detail. Is there somewhere in your body, you can feel this? **What words describe how you are feeling right now?**

At this point, gently squeeze the knuckle of your thumb on your right hand between the thumb and forefinger of your left hand. Keep visualising the small grainy inner critic, and the comical voice, as well as how this makes you feel, and at the same time, keep squeezing your thumb as mentioned above.

Repeat the above as many times as you need to until when you squeeze your right thumb as described, it automatically conjures up the feeling of having your inner critic under control.

> In future, if you ever feel your inner critic is getting a little out of control and having more influence in your mind than you would like. **Then simply squeeze the knuckle of your thumb on your right hand to instantly transform it** into that small comical image, with a squeaky voice and the feeling that comes with that.
>
> Take your time with this and enjoy the process. You have total control of how your inner critic looks and sounds.

At the start of this chapter, I mentioned that my inner critic is Trog. It goes back to a film I watched at a drive-in movie theatre in Australia when I was a child. I was probably about four years old at the time. The film is a 1970 creation and is laughable now, but when I was so young, my imagination ran riot. If you do want to laugh at an old movie, then you could do much worse than check out Trog.

I thought Trog was a fitting inner critic as he had haunted me through a period of my childhood when I had nightmares and hid under the covers waiting for Trog to appear. I enjoyed the exercise of shrinking him down to the size of my thumb and imagine him holding on for dear life on my shoelaces as I flick him off when he tries to take control.

For all these years, you have let your inner critic control how you see and hear it. Now you have taken back control and can see and hear your inner critic for what it is. Are you seriously going to take any notice of that ridiculous sounding, tiny, caricatured inner critic again?

You are in control, you have control over your inner critic and how much power you decide to let it have. It is your mind, so assert your authority over it. When your inner critic next gives you unsolicited advice or starts to make you feel bad about yourself. Stop, breathe and then squeeze the knuckle of your right thumb between the thumb and forefinger of your left hand.

If this does not bring back the feeling of control, then you may need to repeat exercise 3 onwards to embed that feeling.

Your relationship with your inner critic should be transformed and have you firmly back in control.

Quick Quiz:

Questions
1. What two strategies are used in this chapter to tame your inner critic?
2. What is the reframing technique based on?
3. Using 'the acknowledging' your inner critic technique. What should you view your inner critic as?

Answers
1.
2.
3.

Bring On Your Cheerleader

What do I mean by a cheerleader? A dictionary definition I found states a cheerleader is an enthusiastic and vocal supporter of someone or something.

You have had your inner critic hanging around for most of your life and taking up valuable thought space. In the last chapter Taming your Inner Critic, you reduced your inner critic's influence in shaping your thoughts.

However, that creates a bit of a vacuum, and you do not want to invite your inner critic back in, so how can you fill this vacuum in an empowering way?

You can create your inner cheerleader, a polar opposite to your inner critic. Look at exercise 1 and create your inner cheerleader now.

Exercise 1:

Create your Cheerleader.

Picture someone you admire; they could be living, dead or even fictional.

It is personal to you. It could be a family member or a superhero as long as they resonate with you.

You may have shrunk your inner critic down to size, but you still need to fill that vacuum. When you next ask yourself some challenging questions, your cheerleader and not your inner critic can show up.

Who are you going to nominate to be your cheerleader?

My cheerleader is:

Your cheerleader should be an empowering figure and someone or something which fills you with confidence and the 'I can do it' feeling when you hear them speak.

Of course, this will not feel natural at first, but if every time you catch yourself asking a question in your mind, visualise your cheerleader answering instead of your inner critic. You could even picture your cheerleader knocking your inner critic aside as they take over the show.

Keep practising, and in time it will become second nature. Think about that for a moment. Wherever you are in the world, you can summon your hero, icon, whoever they are at will to answer your question positively.

Like any habit, it needs constant practise to become established. You were not born with an inner critic, it developed in early childhood, and its influence has grown over time. There is no reason you can not adopt an inner cheerleader now and let it grow over time and take the place of your inner critic.

A client of mine went through some of these exercises and found them powerful and transformational. I have to say she really applied herself to the process and held nothing back.

Unfortunately, my client's mum had passed away a few years ago, which was hard on her, not to mention many other issues that were happening to her at the time.

It was fascinating to hear that she chose her mum as her cheerleader and found that powerful and reassuring. I thought that was a beautiful and powerful way to create and use your inner cheerleader.

The reason I mentioned my client and her inner cheerleader, is because my inner cheerleader is my dear mother too. Unfortunately, my Mum had an operation in 2011 and suffered complications and passed away not long after, while in intensive care. My parents lived in Australia, and I was in England, but I managed to make the journey in time to say my goodbye's.

The lesson to me was never to take life for granted, never settle for less than you need to. Grab life and embrace it to the full. Life is a gift you are blessed to have, and it can be fragile and unpredictable.

My mum always thought I was a little angel, I was not, but she still saw the best in me. Mum always believed in me and whatever I chose to do. I used to have frequent long chats with my mum over the phone and would often ask her advice, or she would just listen to what was going on in my life at the time.

My Mum was my cheerleader back then, and even though she is no longer in this world, she is in my heart and is my inner cheerleader to this day.

ASKING BETTER QUESTIONS

Asking the wrong type of questions is an invite for your inner critic to show up.

I do not know about you, but I have often fallen into the trap of asking myself the wrong type of questions.

Questions that will tend to get a negative answer. I am thinking of questions like:
- Why does this always happen to me?
- Why can I not stick to this diet?
- Why am I no good at this?
- Why am I always late?
- Why are the traffic lights always red for me?
- Why can I not learn this?

- Why is life so difficult?

Exercise 2:

Have you got some examples of disempowering questions like those mentioned? Get them out in the open and **write them down**.

Notice something similar in all the example questions?

They all begin with Why? How about asking more empowering questions like:
- How can I make sure this does not happen again?
- What can I do to make sure this does not happen again?
- How could I make this diet easier?
- What could I change about myself or the diet to make it successful?
- How could I get better at this?
- What would I need to do to improve this?
- What could I learn from this?
- How can I learn from this?
- What can I do to make sure I am never late?
- How could I make sure I am not late next time?
- What time do I need to set off, to give myself plenty of time, in case I run into some red lights?
- What could I do to break this learning down into smaller chunks so that I can digest it easily?
- How can I make my life easier?
- What things can I do to make my life easier?

In the more empowering questions, you should focus more on what and how type questions.

Ask your brain a question, and it will quickly look to find an answer. Asking questions like 'why am I no good at this?' will usually end up with instant negative responses, such as 'because you are useless'. Ask a disempowering question, and your brain can quickly fire back a stock disempowering answer. Asking yourself a disempowering question assumes that there is a problem which can not be solved, that you are the root of the problem and that there is only one way to solve the problem. You have put yourself into a negative, unproductive state.

However, asking a more empowering question puts your brain into a more in-depth problem-solving mode enabling you to find a solution instead of a negative stock answer. This way, your mind can search for solutions to the problem in ways you may not have thought of before. Let your brain be creative. Your mind is unique and outstanding at finding answers to your questions.

If the answer that comes back is not one you are happy with, either ask the question again, looking for another solution or ask a different question, such as 'What else could I do instead?'.

Asking empowering questions means you are taking back control of the direction you want to go in life rather than letting life's bumpy path dictate to you where to go. Thereby serving you better and moving you forward in your life.

Ask a question which needs a solution such as How can I, or What could I do to and your brain goes into a problem-solving state. When in a problem-solving mode, your mind will try to come up with a great answer to solve your problem. Unlike a disempowering stock answer, you may have to wait a little longer for the answer to arrive. Still, it will be a solution or something to help you move toward a solution rather than just a throwaway negative answer.

> **Exercise 3:**
>
> Look at the questions you wrote down in Exercise 2. How could you change them to **make them more empowering questions**, like the what and how questions?
>
> Every time you catch yourself asking a disempowering question, **stop, and think how can I make this an empowering question instead**? Keep doing this, and it will become second nature to you in no time.

My challenge to you is the next time you catch yourself asking a disempowering question. Stop! Deep Breathe. Change it around to make it an empowering question instead, as you have done in the previous exercises.

Like everything, this will take some time and practice. But listen out for the whys or that emotion that makes you feel unsure, doubtful or fearful. If you have such a feeling, try to think what prompted it and flip it around to a more empowering question or statement.

Sometimes, there may be things in life which are not a good fit for you and your skills. The question to ask may not always be 'How could I improve my skills in this area?'. Instead, you may need to ask a different type of question such as 'What other jobs would my skills be more suitable for?'.

A great quote about questions:

"Successful people ask better questions, and as a result, they get better answers."
Tony Robbins

Let's face it life is a journey and a bumpy one at that. Things do not always go your way, and that is part and parcel of life. When things do not go as planned for me, one of my favourite questions I like to ask myself is: **What can I learn from this?** Then if the same situation occurs in the future, I have a better solution to handle it.

Another great idea when asking yourself empowering questions is to let your imagination run away with itself. Get creative. It may feel a little strange at first, and you may without thinking dismiss some of the answers you get back from empowering questions you ask.

For example, you may need an extra injection of money, so you ask the question, how can I get more money? Your brain comes back with an imaginative answer 'rob a bank'. Before you discard the creative but unlawful solution, it can lead to other thoughts which are related and useful. You may start asking, how can a bank help me? Your brain comes back with responses such as a bank loan or overdraft.

The example above is one which is possible if your circumstances fit. My message to you is, do not instantly dismiss creative answers which do not fit in with reality, but instead pull on the answer a little more, asking what else I could do? Quite often, your mind will make connections which will be relevant and serve you.

Apart from the questions, you have already covered in this chapter, here are some other empowering questions, which could help you come to a solution to a current challenge.

- Who else needs to be involved in this?
- Who do I know who has some experience of this?
- What could I do differently to make this work?
- What is right with what I am currently doing?
- What would (insert the name of someone you admire) do in this situation?
- What is the most useful thing I can focus on right now?
- How will I know when what I am doing is working?
- How will I know when it is complete?
- What is the next best thing I can do?
- How can I use this current challenge to my advantage?
- How can I break this down into more manageable tasks?
- What can I do right now that will move me forward just a little?

I have come up with some empowering questions to get you started, which are only limited by your imagination. It is a great habit to get into, to practice asking empowering questions, and you will be surprised by how powerful the results can be.

Exercise 4:

What empowering questions can you come up with on your own?

Quick Quiz:

Questions
1. What has your inner critic left, that you can fill with your inner cheerleader?
2. What mode will your brain go into when you ask an empowering question?
3. What do successful people ask, which gets them better answers?

Answers
1.
2.
3.

Your Inner Circle

Jim Rohn said: ***"You are the average of the five people you spend the most time with"***.

Based on the statement above, I want you to jump straight into an exercise.

Exercise 1:

Who are the five people you spend the most time with?

1.
2.
3.
4.
5.

Your relationships with friends and family can significantly influence the choices you make in life. For instance, your friends can be a significant influence in helping you resist a temptation like a large purchase or even a cake. They could be a considerable influence on inspiring you to exercise more and become more healthy.

However, they are just as likely to end up encouraging you to give in to temptation and have that chocolate bar, that next drink or give your gym session a miss.

You are most likely to start behaving in similar ways to the friends who surround you. Have you got friends who make poor choices in their lives? Or are your friends the kind who inspire you and enable you to have a much greater chance of reaching your goals?

It all depends on the friends you choose to have around you. As well as affecting your choices in life (many times subconsciously), your friends also have a significant impact on how you think and feel about yourself.

How your friends and family think about you, and react to you, has a significant impact on your perception of yourself. If a partner or close friend already sees you in a good light, like the person you are aspiring to be, that will have a positive impact on your self-perception. But the reverse is also true. If that same partner or close friend had a more negative view of you, this could affect who you ultimately become in a negative sense.

Because your friends and family have such a powerful impact on how you see yourself this can encourage your inner critic, to the extent, your inner critic may quote what a 'friend' said to prevent you taking action.

Despite your friends having such a massive influence over your life, many of your friendships may not have formed by conscious choice. What I mean by this, is in the cold light of day, an ideal friend should share your values (but that does not mean you have to agree on everything). You can have shared values but differing opinions. An ideal friend will always have your best interests at heart and be supportive. Taking this along with how your close friends and family can impact your sense of self, it is so important to start thinking about how you choose your friends wisely.

As a friend yourself, you should have your own friend's best interests at heart and be supportive in helping them to attain their goals. You should be a giver in your friendship and aim to have friends that reciprocate in giving back. At different times in your friendships, you will need to both give and take, and that is a healthy balance to have. It is friends that are predominantly takers who are not beneficial to be around for too long.

Having close friends can have a significant impact on your health. Studies have shown that intimate friendships are known to reduce stress, blood pressure and even cholesterol. Sometimes it may feel that your close friends are causing your stress, but over the long term, the benefits outweigh the downside.

Especially as you get older, having a close friend to confide in can make a world of difference to not only your quality of life but also your longevity especially if you have an extensive network of friends, compared to those who do not.

Just like Jim Rohn's quote at the beginning of this chapter, over many years, I have seen the same type of quotes from many quarters. In essence, the message is this:

If you are trying to become a particular type of person or reach a specific goal, then you should surround yourself with those that are already that type of person

or who have already achieved that goal or are on that same journey themselves.

If you are surrounding yourself with others who look up to you, and when you compare your life to theirs, it makes you feel good because you feel like your life is more significant than theirs, then all you are serving is your ego!

It is excellent if you want to serve others and help them climb their ladders of success, but they should not be the majority of the people in your circle. I have also heard the quote which I think re-iterates my earlier point.
"If you are the most significant person in the room, then you're in the wrong room."
Rich Litvin

Which seems to be closely related to the quote from Confucius,
"If you're the smartest person in the room, then you're in the wrong room".

If you want to keep growing as a person and professional in your field, then it is essential to level up your peer group. Take the example of a tennis pro. If the tennis pro continues to hang out and play against mediocre players, then it will massage their ego but will not improve their game as they are not being challenged enough. However if they level up and mainly play against players better than themselves, then they will be out of their comfort zone, it will stretch their abilities and they will have to adapt and change their game to level up. By surrounding themselves with better players, they will also learn the tips and techniques of those same players, and it will improve their tennis game.

So, whatever you want to achieve in life, try to be near those that have already arrived there. Most will be happy if you are serious, to give you shortcuts, thereby avoiding some costly mistakes along the way. Just being around this peer group, will help push you and enable you to attain a higher level. Your ego will not be in charge, you will be out of your comfort zone, and stretch yourself to the limit, but most of all you will grow!

One caveat to a peer group who have attained what you want to achieve in the future is work with those that are a few steps ahead of you, rather than too far ahead. You want to be inspired not to have your confidence knocked and similarly for those in the group, if they are a few steps ahead of you, they will be happy to help as it was not so long ago that they were in your place.

I'm sure you have all had people in your inner circle that you are excited to be around and who motivate and inspire you. Those that make life seem that much more exciting and are a definite asset to your inner circle. They are natural givers and seem to create excitement in you, which almost feels like you are a battery, and they are helping to top up your charge. These people need to be nurtured and encouraged to be part of your inner circle.

Conversely, you have probably also all had the experience of people in your inner circle who are self-obsessed. There can be at least two types of people in this category. Some want to show off and be adored by everyone else in their circle, but give little in the way of any value back. Some just see the world in a negative light, whatever happens. I am not talking about those suffering from depression or going through troubles, as we can all be negative during those times.

I am talking about the people for as long as you have known them, know how to put a negative spin on everything. Having people like these in your inner circle is draining as they want so much attention but give nothing back. Looking at the battery metaphor again, these people drain your battery. These type of people are takers, and you want to trim them from your inner circle or at least limit your exposure to them where you can.

Exercise 2:

Who in your inner circle drains your energy when you are around them?

What could you do, to limit your time around them or if needed, drop them from your circle?

Exercise 3:

Who in your inner circle leaves you feeling inspired, excited and gives you energy?

What could you do to spend more time with them?

How could you increase the number of people like this in your circle?

As I mentioned earlier, your inner circle has a profound effect on your life, as you tend to reflect the attributes of the people you are around the most.

It is easy to see how you can become more like the person you aspire to be, by spending more time with those who have already walked the walk of the journey you are currently on or are at least a few steps ahead.

It follows then, if you want to be more confident, hang out with people who are more confident than you, learn from them and see how they behave in different situations. Share with them that you are aiming to be more confident like them, most will be flattered and only too willing to help you on your journey.

Of course, this does not apply just to confidence; it applies across the board to all manner of things. For example, if you want to be healthier, then aim to spend more time with healthier people, and the list goes on as far as you can imagine.

The above examples are personal attributes you may want to work on and improve. All of this carries over to the business world too, and the people you should look to spend more time around are the people who are already doing what you want to achieve in business or your career.

Of course, you can not always get the inner circle of your dreams, as some of the people may be unavailable to you. What you can do, however, is look at what these people consume as their media. You get a feel for some of the content they receive, which may help you get inspired in your chosen field.

Beyond that, if the person you are aspiring to be like creates social media content, then if you can, subscribe to that. They can be like a virtual mentor to you, and you can benefit from their experiences, tips and tricks.

Social media like it or loathe it, you are in a connected world, and social media is not going away any time soon. Virtually the same rules apply to your social media feed and the content you consume as in the real world. However, on social media, you can be a little more ruthless with your culling of takers and energy drainers. If they are friends or family members that you can not or do not want to cut from your life, you have the option of unfollowing them, so their content does not end up in your news feed, and they will be none the wiser.

If you can not help comparing yourself to others on social media and it starts to harm your mental well being, then I would encourage you to unfollow the people involved.
Also, try to limit your social media consumption if you can.

One brilliant way of controlling social media consumption is to try out the following exercise.

Exercise 4:

Have you heard of a food diary before? Well, now, I want you to **create a social media diary.** For a week (including weekends) **log all the time you currently spend on social media.**

How did you feel during the time you were on social media and immediately when you came off? Did you start to compare yourself to others and their experiences? Only your eyes will see this, so be honest with yourself.

After completing exercise 4, move on to exercise 5, to finalise your results for the week.

Exercise 5:

Total minutes spent on social media for the week:

Describe a summary of your feelings from your social media use for the week:

Looking at the amount of time you have spent on social media this week, is there something else you could have done with that time, that may have had a more positive impact on your life, if so what is it?

After completing exercise 5, you may be shocked by the amount of time you have been spending on social media. Could you spend your time more productively? Here are some strategies for helping you to be effective with your social media time.

I know in the past, I have struggled with a lively social media feed and FOMO (fear of missing out) and reacting to notifications throughout the day, which distracted me from other tasks. I had to assess what was more critical, making an intentional effort to achieve something of value or reacting to a notification like Pavlov's dogs to a bell. Fortunately, I could step back and assess my social media use and turn off my notifications, so I could then complete tasks without distraction and go back to social media at a time of my choosing.

How to be more effective with your use of social media:

- **Turn off your social media notifications.** Social media is not designed for your convenience and benefit. It is for the use of the social media platform itself, and it's advertisers. They want your eyes on them as much as possible. The more time they can get you to spend on the platform, the more advertising they can put in front of you, which in turn means, the more profit they make.
- **Timebox some social media time.** What I mean by this, is to schedule some time for your social media use each day. Rather than social media controlling your schedule, you are taking back control. Then you can spend the amount of time you would have spent on social media being more productive.

One quote I love that sums up what can happen when you are comparing yourself to others on social media.

"The reason why we struggle with insecurity is because we compare our behind the scenes with everyone else's highlight reel."
Stephen Furtick

Quick Quiz:

Questions
1. How many people are you the average of, that you spend the most time with?
2. If you want to be more confident, then hang out with people that are?
3. Name one way of controlling the use of social media?

Answers
1.
2.
3.

Confidence Builder

You have looked at your story and then gone on to listen to your inner critic and name them. From there, you shrunk your inner critic down to size and made them insignificant. You brought on your cheerleader and are now looking at asking yourself better questions.

If you are still here at this point, then I can tell, you are serious about dealing with your inner critic and that you are someone who steps up and takes action when they need to.

One way of consolidating your gains is to give yourself credit when you have had a breakthrough, learned something new or had a win.

I bet you can be hard on yourself at times. It is crucial that no matter how small the breakthrough, lesson learned, or win, you need to acknowledge it as another step along your journey. These micro acknowledgements will build up over time, but you must record them, so you do not forget.

Exercise 1:

Write down some small wins, breakthroughs or lessons learnt in the past week.

Exercise 2:

Write down some small wins, breakthroughs or lessons learnt in the past month.

Now you have created your recent win list from the last week and month, it is essential these wins get the acknowledgement they deserve. Exercise 3 is just the way to do that.

Exercise 3:

I want you to go on a visual journey inside your head. Close your eyes and imagine venturing deep inside your mind, until you come to a door. It is a beautiful door, just the type you would pick. You open the door and step inside the room.

Your confidence room, it is full of your trophies, badges, medals and certificates, and they are ordered chronologically from when you were a toddler to the present time. As you look around the room, it is breathtaking and decorated in just the way you would like it. It feels comfortable, safe and relaxing.

The room seems to extend for some way, and there are certificates, medals and trophies as far as the eye can see. **Just stepping into this room fills you with immense pride and confidence as these are all your achievements**.

Walking by some of your early achievements, such as taking your first steps; uttering your first words; reading your first book; tying your shoelaces for the first time and even riding your bike without training wheels.

Looking back now as an adult, these may not look like significant achievements. Still, at one time, you had to use all your courage and determination to make these things happen. You quickly forget the achievement once

> you have mastered a skill. **It is good to acknowledge just how far you've come on your journey**.
>
> As you walk further inside, you see all manner of wins throughout your life, both large and small. Finally, you get to a part of the room where there is space to display more of your successes.
>
> **Now it is time to take each of your wins from the last week and month**, one at a time and decide what shape the award will take. Will it merit a certificate, a medal or a trophy or something else altogether, the choice is yours. Once you have decided on the award, then place the award where you can see it next time you walk into your confidence room. These are your latest wins and will be easy to spot when you next come in.
>
> After you have acknowledged all your current wins, slowly walk back through the room and **see all the achievements of your life**. There should be many more than you initially remembered. **These are moments from your life that you should be proud of, and you need to celebrate them**.
>
> Finally, you come back to the door. **You have a sense of confidence and pride**, and rightly so, that's a big room you have started to fill, and there are many more wins to come in the future too. You open the door and open your eyes.

After creating your confidence room; you need to visit it regularly and appreciate what you have achieved in your life to date. Enjoy watching your confidence room grow in size to accommodate all your achievements.

On days when things are not working out, revisit your confidence room and realise that you are much more than the problems that today brings. Visiting your confidence room can help you to build your confidence. It will allow you to be brave when stepping outside your comfort zone, as you have all the evidence of your past wins.

Exercise 4:

The point of this exercise is to make sure you continuously note down all your daily or at least weekly achievements. **It does not matter how small; they are all critical.**

Record every small win each day and week, so that you can then add them to your confidence room at least once a week.

Then every time you achieve something new, **enjoy visiting your confidence room** and placing your new achievement in the perfect place.

Another way of building your confidence in increments is a method similar to your confidence room; only this one is not virtual. Here is a daily exercise where you write down at least one win a day.

Exercise 5:

Daily Wins Book.

For this exercise, **you will need a notebook**. I call mine, my daily wins book, but use a name which feels right for you.

The idea behind this is that every day you record at least one win, no matter how small. There will be days where you feel you have not achieved anything, but maybe that day has helped you learn something either about yourself or a current challenge which will help you in the future. **Learning something new is a definite win**.

A quote I love about this is:
"Sometimes you win, and sometimes you learn."
John C. Maxwell

Other times the win might be that you have rested your body through some injury, but that is what your body needs at this time, and you are wise enough to heed your body's request.

No matter what the day throws at you, **there can always be a win somewhere** in there, and sometimes you just have to dig a little deeper to find it.

As mentioned before, enter a win for each day of the week. Then at the end of the week, review them and **write down what you have learnt about yourself** and how you feel when reading those wins back.

> It is not important if these are small wins, as that is mainly the point. **Building up plenty of small wins consistently over time**, to help you realise you can have at least one success a day even on your worst days. Over time **this will train your mind to seek out wins automatically** and thereby building your confidence.
>
> At the end of each month, review your weekly summary notes and write down what you have learnt about yourself and how that makes you feel.
>
> You always need to be training yourself to reflect on your wins. Too often, you can be quick to rush to judgement about yourself when something goes wrong. This exercise is all about establishing both the habit and to train your brain to seek out the wins of each day, week, month and year.

Now in various ways, you have started to appreciate your successes and build on them. By doing that, you are also building up your confidence. But do not get stuck being confident in your comfort zone. You need to stretch your abilities; otherwise, you will not grow as a person.

So look at exercise 6, which I think is a fun way to stretch yourself out of your comfort zone just a little at a time, until your stretch zone starts to become your new comfort zone.

Exercise 6:

Stretch Jar

For this exercise, you will need a jar, box or similar, which you can easily fit your hand inside. Next, take some strips of paper (this may take some time as you will have to get creative with ideas, but it is well worth persisting with).

On each strip of paper, write down something like a **small task that would feel slightly uncomfortable** for you to do, but not fill you with fear, **taking just small steps to build momentum**.

Also add some slips of paper in, with **some fun things to do** written on them, something that you can enjoy either on your own or with others. **Life should have room for some fun**, after all.

How about adding in some slips of paper with things that you have meant to get around to, but you never quite find the time (before adding these, make sure you want or need to do these things). These could be things on your to-do list which are not urgent and seem to get copied across from list to list.

If there are some important goals you have in life, then write down the **first small step you would need to take**, so you are one step closer to that goal.

Fold all these bits of paper up, so you can not read what is on them unless you unfold them. Put them all in your jar/box. Mix them up with your hand.

Each day, take one slip of paper from the jar/box read

> what is on it and commit to following through on that one task at some point during your day. These should only be small tasks and not too demanding to carry out.
>
> **Reflect** on whether you carried out the task or not; if you did **give yourself credit** for completing today's assignment. Now you have to come up with another item to replace it. If today's mission was toward a more significant project, then what is the next small step you need to take, to move closer toward the goal? Write it down and put it back in the jar/box and mix them up again. If you are writing in your daily wins book, then make an entry about your **success, in completing the task**.
>
> If you did not manage to complete today's task and did not even start it, fold the paper back up and put it back in the jar/box and mix it in with all the other items. If you did start the task but not complete it, then **reflect on why that is**. Was the job too big, does it need to be broken down further? If it does, you know what to do and where to put these smaller tasks.
>
> If however, you have nearly completed the task, but not entirely, then take it over into the next day to complete. Never move it beyond one day, if it is still not complete, it should go back in the jar/box, ready to be picked out again in the future.
>
> **At the end of the week if you've completed at least five of the tasks you have picked out, then make sure you give yourself a treat or reward. You've earned it.**

I have found that over time acknowledging all my little wins and especially writing them down, gives me a real sense of achievement. I know like many other people I am guilty of glossing over any small and sometimes large achievements.

Over the years, I have written down my small wins, including recording them on apps. Most successfully for me when I was using a running app on my phone. Seeing the miles increase gave me a real sense of achievement over time and a belief in myself that I was capable of doing more. You could even have it linked to your Facebook account, while you were on your run, you would hear a cheer if people liked your post, which was a real boost.

At the end of the run, the app would have a trainer speak and congratulate you on how you had done. Especially true if you had broken a personal best time or distance, which made me want to up my game. If you are into your technology, it may be worth investing in an app to help you track your small wins, such as a habit tracking app.

When it comes to acknowledging where I fall short, then I could be a master of that. That is why it is essential to embrace all your wins in life. Ever heard the saying 'bad news sells'? Well, your brain is pre-programmed to look for the negative in life because, in the distant past, it meant danger and was a warning sign.

It's easy for you to take negative things others say to you to heart. In the past, this could have been a survival tactic, as it was essential to fit in with your tribe as being cast out from the tribe would almost certainly have been a death sentence. Humans also seem predisposed to seeing the worst in ourselves too.

Reprogramming yourself to celebrate even your smallest wins can be a significant confidence boost, especially if you build this into a long-term habit.

Quick Quiz:

Questions
1. What can you give yourself when you have had a breakthrough?
2. In what type of room did you store your wins?
3. Complete the sentence. 'Sometimes you win and ….'?

Answers
1.
2.
3.

Reflection

Thank you for spending your hard-earned money on this book. I appreciate the trust you have put in me to help lessen the influence of your inner critic in your life.

I hope you have taken the time to go through all the exercises thoroughly as it is only by fully taking part that you will notice the change in your thinking and confidence. Even then this is something which you need to practise until you no longer have to think about it consciously and it just becomes part of who you are.

I want you to be successful in taming your inner critic, and I hope you feel you have grown as a result.

You have been on quite the journey and have discovered the stories you tell yourself along the way. Stories that had become so ingrained that you accept them as fact and never challenged them. Now you are armed with the knowledge and tools to dismantle any story you have created, that does not serve you.

You have seen how labels can be all too easily accepted and given without much thought. You are now in control of what labels you wish to give yourself or receive from others as well as those you give to others.

It was essential to understand where your inner critic came from, how your childhood was the birthplace of your inner critic and how it assumed more power over time. That childhood inner critic is no longer relevant to your adult life and is only holding you back from your potential.

Imposter syndrome is rife in our society, and if you suffer from it, then you were able to see which category of imposter you were most like and understand the strategies needed to reduce the imposter feeling.

You focussed on listening in on your inner critic enabling you to work out the common phrases that your inner critic comes up with time and again. Once you were able to recognise these, you then had the power to work on them and remove the leverage it gives your inner critic.

One of my favourite parts of the book is Taming your Inner Critic. When you finally get to come face to face with your inner critic. At this point, you start to realise you can take back control and see your inner critic for what it is.

Bringing on your Inner Cheerleader is where you filled the vacuum, your inner critic left and created a positive force to enjoy whenever you need it.

Your inner circle is crucial to your success in life. Now you are aware of that fact; you can grow your inner circle in a pro-active way, and help cultivate your success.

Finally, you went through the confidence builder, which helps to boost your inner cheerleader, and you saw how to build your confidence from recognising and acknowledging little wins along your journey.

In the following exercises, I want to ensure you embed the most important lessons of the book.

Exercise 1:

What name did you give to your inner critic?

What does your inner critic sound like now?

Describe your inner critic (how they appear to you now) in detail.

Exercise 2:

What is the name of your inner cheerleader?

Describe your inner cheerleader in detail.

Exercise 3:

What wins have you had as a direct result of reading this book?

Which method do you prefer to record your wins, the confidence room or the daily wins book? (Both is a valid answer too.)

Before this book, I had written an ebook, which was an abbreviated version of what you see and only covered five areas of how to tame your inner critic. But even that ebook had a profound effect on some people's lives, which they fed back to me. It was at that point I knew I had to get the full version of the book published and out into the world so that I can impact many more lives out there.

Reflecting on the exercises you have completed in this book, what have you learnt about yourself that you were not aware of before?

Exercise 4:

What have I learnt about myself on my journey through this book?

Detailed Quiz:

Questions
1. What is the preconscious?
2. What part of the personality deals with the reality principle?
3. What part of your personality is the inner critic?
4. Cortisol is also known as the ...... hormone?
5. What type of figure should your inner cheerleader be?
6. Disempowering questions often start with what word?
7. What two words are often at the start of empowering questions?
8. If you ask better questions, then you get better ....?
9. How big do your wins have to be to build your confidence over time?
10. What type of room can you store your wins in?
11. How many types of imposter syndrome are there?
12. Name one of the types of imposter syndrome.
13. Approximately what percentage of people are affected by imposter syndrome at some point in their lives?
14. Reframing the way your inner critic speaks to you could be done as a compassionate ......?
15. What breathing technique can change your state and help to distract you from negative thoughts?
16. What is the metaphor that discusses bubbles called?
17. What two techniques can you use to tame your inner critic?
18. The labels you give yourself should be .... and not ....
19. You are the average of how many people?
20. What are two ways you can limit your use of social media?

Answers
1.
2.
3.
4.
5.
6.
7.
8.
9.
10.
11.
12.
13.
14.
15.
16.
17.
18.
19.
20.

Quiz Question Answers

Introduction

Answers
1. Every experience in life, good or bad, is something you can learn from, to help you grow.
2. Elon Musk
3. An active reader

Your Story

Answers
1. Our story
2. Negative

The Importance We Attach To Labels

Answers
1. Impact
2. Respect
3. Can limit what perceive you are capable of doing

Where Did My Inner Critic Come From

Answers
1. Id, ego and superego
2. Id
3. Ideal self and conscience

Imposter Syndrome

Answers:
1. Dr Valerie Young
2. The Natural Genius
3. Others

Listening In On Your Inner Critic

Answers:
1. Comfort zone
2. 4 7 8 breathing technique
3. Transient

Taming Your Inner Critic

Answers:
1. Acknowledge your inner critic and reframe your inner critic
2. Neuro-Linguistic Programming

3. A frightened little child

Bring On Your Cheerleader

Answers:
1. A vacuum
2. Problem-solving
3. Better questions

Your Inner Circle

Answers:
1. Five
2. Confident
3. Turn off social media notifications

Confidence Builder

Answers:
1. Credit
2. Confidence room
3. Sometimes you learn

Reflection

Answers:
1. Contains everything that can be brought into the conscious mind.
2. The ego
3. Superego
4. Stress
5. An empowering figure
6. Why
7. What and How
8. Answers
9. Small
10. Confidence room
11. 5
12. Any of these is correct (Perfectionist, Superman/Superwoman, Natural Genius, Soloist and Expert)
13. 70%
14. Friend
15. 4 7 8 breathing technique
16. The bubble machine
17. Acknowledge your inner critic and Reframing your inner critic
18. Empowering and not disempowering
19. 5
20. Turn off notifications and timebox social media time

About The Author

I'm Michael Garde. I'm a Personal Performance Coach,
and the founder of MG Performance Coaching.

I live with my lovely wife Kerry and our two cats Daisy and Paisley.

I'm a proud father of two beautiful daughters and one step-daughter. I'm also a proud Grandad of six grandchildren.

I would love to hear if this book has made a difference to your life.

Please contact me by email:
mike@mgperformancecoaching.com

Join my private Facebook group:
www.facebook.com/groups/themindsetguy/

Visit my website and join my mailing list:
www.mgperformancecoaching.com

Free resources will be added for you to download from:
www.mgperformancecoaching.com/tameyourinnercritic

Printed in Great Britain
by Amazon